RESPONDING TO GOD

MARCH 28 - MARY'S
APRIL 18 - Ron &
BETTY'S

RESPONDING TO GOD

A GUIDE TO DAILY PRAYER

MARTHA GRAYBEAL ROWLETT

UPPER
ROOM BOOKS
NASHVILLE

(Copyright information continued on page 157)

Cover Photograph: Angel Falls, Venezuela (Courtney Milne/MASTERFILE)
Cover Design: Jim Bateman
Interior Design and Layout: Nancy Cole
First Printing: October 1996

Library of Congress Cataloging-in-Publication Data:
Rowlett, Martha Graybeal.
Responding to God: A Guide to Daily Prayer / by Martha Graybeal Rowlett.
    p. cm.
Includes bibliographical references.
1. Prayer—Christianity. I. Title
BV215.R69 1996   96-16354
248.3'2—dc20
CIP
ISBN: 0-8358-0783-5

The mission of Upper Room books is to provide resources that help persons grow in their relationship with God.

for
Robert James Arnott
my husband and friend

and for
the Congregation of the Rolling Hills United Methodist Church,
Rolling Hills Estates, California,
our church family while this book was being written

PREFACE

*I*n my first appointment to a parish as an associate minister, I was responsible for preparing many of the prayers for the Sunday morning worship service. This was my first experience with leading prayer for a congregation on a regular basis. I was forced to confront the poverty of my own experience with prayer. To me prayer was something to do on the spur of the moment, either to thank God for something beautiful or pleasant that had just been experienced, or to send out a call for help in time of trouble when no other solution seemed readily available. This was not exactly what was called for on Sunday mornings in formal worship time for a congregation.

I began researching the experience of prayer in the Christian church. I discovered a rich and wonderful tradition that somehow had escaped my attention in seminary. Preparing to lead the congregation in prayer became a significant time of personal spiritual growth for me. Before long, I discovered that the way one prays grows out of the way one thinks about God. My growth in the life and experience of prayer was putting pressure on my theology. So I began to research contemporary ways of thinking about God.

The most helpful resources for this pilgrimage came from the writings of Dr. John Cobb at the School of Theology at Claremont, especially from his book, *God and the World.*

I was fortunate later to have an opportunity to work with Dr. Cobb in writing a theology of prayer as part of my project for the Doctor of Ministry degree at Claremont. Dr. Howard Clinebell, my other faculty advisor, was also helpful in shaping this material, especially from the psychological point of view. Materials at the core of that project were published by The Upper Room in 1982 under the title *In Spirit and in Truth: A Guide to Praying*. For purposes of the Pathways series, these materials have been revised and expanded for this book.

I have become increasingly impressed with the importance of prayer in the Christian life. Jesus prayed frequently, often for long hours at a time. His ministry was obviously shaped by his time at prayer. Prayer was an important factor in the life of the early church. Prayer played a significant role in the life of John Wesley, who prayed for long periods of time each day.

The "spur-of-the-moment" prayer with which almost everyone is familiar is important, of course. It reflects a consciousness that all of life is lived in God's presence. But this "on-the-run" prayer does not expose one to the range of prayer experience that is part of our tradition. The spiritual life of those who pray in this more intentional way benefits from added richness.

This book is intended for the novice in prayer who wants to learn to pray. It is also for the person who already prays, but who is interested in learning about the wide spectrum of prayer experience in the tradition of the church, and in expanding and deepening a personal experience of prayer.

The book can be used as a study resource for a group interested in exploring the basics of prayer. It can also be read fruitfully by an individual.

The contents of this book have been significantly shaped by the dialogue on prayer that has taken place in classes and workshops and retreats on prayer that I have led over the years. My deepest appreciation goes out to those who have been a part of that dialogue, sharing their own pilgrimage in prayer.

Contents

INTRODUCTION TO PRAYER AND PRAYING   1

*M*illions of people everyday are entering into conversation with God from their bedrooms, their back yards, or their cars." So reported the *Los Angeles Times* in an article that surveyed the practice of prayer among residents of that city and noted that prayer is both controversial and popular in America today.

We debate about public prayer. At the same time the Gallup pollsters report that more than one in three Americans pray about once a day. And books on prayer are increasing in popularity.

Prayer seems to come naturally and easily to most people, while at the same time it raises profound and difficult questions for them.

James Montgomery, in his hymn "Prayer Is the Soul's Sincere Desire" affirms:

> Prayer is the Christian's vital breath,
> The Christian's native air ...
> The upward glancing of an eye
> When none but God is near.

Children learn to pray quickly and often quite creatively. Yet some of the most difficult questions Christians pose for each other come in discussions about prayer.

QUESTIONS PEOPLE ASK ABOUT PRAYER

If you listen to a group talk about prayer, you may hear questions like these:

- How does prayer work?
- Do prayers have to be structured?
- How can we understand unanswered prayer?
- How do you know when God is answering your prayer?
- Is there a right or wrong way to pray?
- To whom do you pray?
- How do you start a prayer?
- Should we expect an answer?
- Is prayer by a group more effective than an individual's prayer?
- Is it okay to pray for everything and anything?
- How do you pray when you haven't been praying regularly and now you have a real need, but you feel guilty asking for God's help when you haven't been consistent in your thanksgiving?
- How do you pray when you are angry at God?
- How do you pray for someone who is dying?

Questions about God as well as feelings about God surface readily in conversations about prayer. Anger at God about unanswered prayers will find expression. Discussion about how to help those you care about through prayer can become intense.

FORMAT FOR THIS STUDY

*T*his study assumes the importance of both praying and thinking about prayer. Unanswered questions about prayer can discourage the regular practice of prayer, while clear and careful thinking about prayer can open a path to a richer and deeper devotional life.

Our minds have been so shaped by the scientific revolution of the past two hundred years that we can be embarrassed and uncomfortable in the face of practices that defy critical scientific analysis. For some people, prayer is a meaningless vestige of the past, existing in the shadowy realm of magic and superstition. They may still go through the motions of prayer, but they are not sure what they are doing. Occasionally the human spirit of the skeptic erupts in prayer in desperate or extreme circumstances.

But the one who prays may not be able to explain or justify the experience to themselves or to anyone else in calmer circumstances. It may be difficult for us to give an account of the faith that is in us. This uncertainty about how to think about prayer may be an inhibition to the life of prayer. Therefore this study provides resources for trying to make sense of our experience of prayer.

Prayer is natural. We are created with the capacity to pray. God gives us the gift of this special communication. We do not have to wait to have a perfectly constructed, carefully analyzed theology of prayer before we begin to pray. We can simply accept the gift and pray.

God has also given us minds with which to analyze our experience. Thinking about prayer is one way to grow in the devotional life. If we have not separated prayer from magic, thinking about prayer can help us do this. If our prayer life is limited to a few memorized prayers learned in childhood, thinking about prayer can open a new world of possibilities. If our prayer life has been frustrating and discouraging, thinking about prayer may help to uncover the problems. There will be unanswered questions, of course, but there can be answered ones too!

But thinking about prayer by itself is not enough. This study also provides structure for the practice of prayer.

Martin Luther once said, "None can believe how powerful prayer is, and what it is able to effect, but those who have learned it by experience." The primary way in which one grows in the life of prayer is by praying. It is possible to talk about prayer, to describe much about it. But our prayers can go where our thoughts cannot follow.

RESOURCES FOR THINKING ABOUT PRAYER

The process of thinking about prayer will use four questions:

1. How can we think about God?
2. How can we think about prayer?
3. How can we pray?
4. What difference does prayer make?

Resources for answering these questions will be drawn from scripture, the tradition of Christian worship, reason, and experience. The scriptures will be from the New Revised Standard Version of the Bible (NRSV). The tradition will come from the hymns and liturgical prayers of the church, and the prayers of some great Christians. The theology will come primarily from the work of John Cobb and David Griffin and their theological ancestor, Alfred North Whitehead. The experience of many people who have written and spoken on the subject of prayer will be interspersed as testimony. Thus, the study is an expression of the Wesleyan quadrilateral of scripture, tradition, reason, and experience.

RESOURCES FOR PRAYING

A pattern for a daily period of prayer is offered in prayer guides at the end of each chapter. The guides are designed to be used for one week. They are intended to provide a format for experiencing a spectrum of ways to pray.

The Spanish mystic Teresa of Avila (1515–1582) said that the best way to pray is the way you pray best. Each of us needs to create an approach that seems natural and that fits where we are. The pattern outlined here reflects centuries of experience in Christian devotion, and yet it is only one of the many possible patterns. The general outline is as follows:

1. Preparation and centering
2. Praise and adoration
3. Confession
4. Meditative reading of scripture
5. Petitions
6. Intercessions
7. Thanksgiving
8. Dedication
9. Silence
10. Benediction

The study begins with thinking about prayer in a general sense and then moves to the "how-to's" of the different ways we can pray. The guides with helps for praying in several different ways are introduced at the beginning to provide opportunity to experience prayer in preparation for reflecting on it later.

Use of the prayer guides assumes a discipline of setting aside private time for prayer. A block of uninterrupted time that can be as brief as fifteen minutes is desirable. A Bible will be needed. A notebook that can serve as a prayer journal may be helpful. In the journal, you can write your thoughts and prayers. This makes it possible to look back over your prayers to see how your prayers have been answered and how your prayers have grown.

The position for praying depends on the person and the circumstances. Kneeling with the head bowed and the eyes closed has been a tradition in Christian worship as a symbol of humility before God. Popular for private worship is the sitting position, in a straight chair with feet flat on the floor. All of the muscles of the body can relax in this position, so it lends itself to stillness and concentration. Some people stand, while others lie down to pray. Reducing sense stimulation by closing the eyes is helpful to many people. Others find that looking at a religious object like a cross or crucifix helps focus their attention.

The guides for daily prayer provided in this study begin with scripture sentences that draw awareness to the presence of God and the purpose of prayer. The prayers are not intended to be complete in themselves. They are starting places for personal prayers. The use of ellipses (. . .) in some of the prayers is symbolic of the open-endedness of all of the prayers and an invitation to "fill in the blanks" with your own prayers. This filling in the blanks can be done in a separate notebook with a page for each day. It is not necessary to write anything. The space can be symbolic of your personal, unwritten, and perhaps even nonverbal prayers.

The prayers in these guides draw heavily on scriptural themes and themes from the traditional liturgies of the church. These themes are expressed in simple, contemporary English. Some of the material has been rephrased from corporate prayers to individual prayers for the person praying alone.

Scripture reading is one of the listening parts of prayer. A passage of scripture will be suggested for meditative reading for each day of the week. The passages listed are chosen as resources in the process of learning to pray and to think about prayer. Read them with the expectation that the Holy Spirit may speak to you. Read until something strikes you. Stop and reflect as you feel led. If you are using a prayer journal, record insights, applications, and nudges from your reflection.

Members of a group studying together may want to pledge to remember each other daily in prayer. You can support and encourage and learn from each other.

Silence is suggested at the end of each period of prayer—a time for resting in God's presence. This may be the most awkward and difficult part of the experience at first, but give it a try. You may find that you like it!

PRAYER IN THE LIFE OF JESUS

*P*rayer in the life of the Christian is rooted in the long tradition and practice of prayer in the life of Jesus. The Gospels report that he prayed in the midst of his ordinary life. He left his disciples and went out alone into the desert early in the morning or up into the mountains at the end of a busy day to pray. He went out into the mountains "and he spent the night in prayer to God" (Luke 6:12) before he chose his disciples. He prayed alone.

Sometimes he took his disciples with him (Luke 9:28; Mark 14:32-33). He prayed for other people. The mothers brought their children to him "that he might lay his hands on them and pray" (Matt. 19:13). He told Peter that he had prayed for him, that his faith might not fail (Luke 22:32). He prayed for his enemies. From the cross, he prayed for those who crucified him, "Father, forgive them; for they do not know what they are doing" (Luke 23:34).

And he prayed for himself. The Gospels record words from the Garden of Gethsemane and from the cross. "Abba, Father, for you all things are possible; remove this cup from me; yet, not what I want, but what you want" (Mark 14:36). "Father, into your hands I commend my spirit!" (Luke 23:46) His followers remembered and preserved teachings that revealed the value of prayer to Jesus. Among the few lessons Jesus taught in the form of a commandment were his instructions to "ask, search, and knock" as reported in Luke.

[Jesus] was praying in a certain place, and after he had finished, one of his disciples said to him, "Lord, teach us to pray, as John taught his disciples." He said to them, "When you pray, say:

Father, hallowed be your name.
Your kingdom come.
Give us each day our daily bread.
And forgive us our sins, for we ourselves forgive
    everyone indebted to us.
And do not bring us to the time of trial."

And he said to them: "Suppose one of you has a friend, and you go to him at midnight and say to him, "Friend, lend me three loaves of bread; for a friend of mine has arrived, and I have nothing to set before him. And he answers from within, "Do not bother me; the door has already been locked, and my children are with me in bed; I cannot get up and give you anything." I tell you, even though he will not get up and give him anything because he is his friend, at least because of his persistence he will get up and give him whatever he needs.

"So I say to you, Ask, and it will be given you, search and you will find; knock, and the door will be opened for you. . . . Is there anyone among you who, if your child asks for a fish, will give a snake instead of a fish? Or if the child asks for an egg, will give a scorpion? If you then, who are evil, know how to give good gifts to your children, how much more will the heavenly Father give the Holy Spirit to those who ask him?"

— Luke 11:1–13

PRAYER IN THE EARLY CHURCH

*P*rayer also played a central role in the life of the early church. The story of the birth of the church begins with a group of men and women gathered in an upper room in prayer (Act 1:12–14). After Pentecost, the new converts "devoted themselves to the apostles' teaching and fellowship, to the breaking of bread and the prayers" (Acts 2:42). The first deacons were appointed to care for the needs of the growing community so that the Twelve could devote themselves to prayer and to the ministry of the word (Acts 6:1–24).

Paul reported that he had been praying for the members of the churches to whom he wrote (1 Thess. 1:2), and he repeatedly asked them to pray for him (1 Thess. 5:25, Rom. 15:30, 2 Cor. 1:11, Col. 4:3). Sometimes this request was open-ended; sometimes it was specific. In prison, Paul spent his time in prayer and "singing hymns to God" (Acts 16:25). In his teachings, he commended the life of prayer. To the church at Philippi, he said, "Do not worry about anything, but in everything by prayer and supplication with thanksgiving let your requests be made known to God" (Phil. 4:6). To the Thessalonians, he said, "Rejoice always, pray without ceasing" (1 Thess. 5:16–17).

A hymn by Arthur Coxe tells the story.

> O where are kings and empires now
> Of old that went and came?
> But, Lord, your church is praying yet,
> A thousand years the same.

This study on prayer is designed to assist those who would keep the practice of prayer alive and healthy in the church.

Preparation and Centering

Be still, and know that I am God![1]

It's me, it's me, it's me, O Lord, standing in the need of prayer.[2]

Praise and Adoration

O God, you are my God, and I long for you.
My whole being desires you;
like a dry, worn-out, and waterless land,
    my soul is thirsty for you.
Let me see you in the sanctuary; let me see
    how mighty and glorious you are.
Your constant love is better than life itself,
    and so I will praise you.
I will give you thanks as long as I live;
I will raise my hands to you in prayer.
My soul will feast and be satisfied, and I will sing
    glad songs of praise to you.[3]

Confession

All have sinned and fallen short of your glory. This is true of me. I confess that I have not lived the way you would have me to live in these ways. . . .

Forgive my sins, O God. Do not remember my wrongs any more. Write your will upon my heart and preserve me among your people.

MEDITATIVE READING OF SCRIPTURES

(Passages reporting on Jesus in prayer)

Day One:	Luke 6:12–16
Day Two:	Mark 14:32–42
Day Three:	Matthew 19:13–15
Day Four:	Luke 11:1–13
Day Five:	Luke 22:31–32
Day Six:	Luke 23:33–35
Day Seven:	Luke 23:44–49

Insights from the scriptures:

PETITIONS (PRAYERS FOR ONESELF)

As Jesus asked for guidance when he had a decision to make, so also I ask for your guidance at this point where I have a decision to make . . .

As Jesus shared with you the pain in his life, so I share with you my pain, asking for relief from suffering . . .

As Jesus taught his disciples to pray, I ask that you teach me to pray . . .

As Jesus trusted you in the most testing times, so I ask you to help me trust your loving care in this difficult situation . . .

I pray for . . .

Intercessions (Prayers for Others)

As Jesus blessed the children, so also I ask your blessing for children. I pray for the children of the world, with all of their potential and vulnerability, that they may be blessed. I pray specifically for these children . . .

As Jesus prayed for his friends, so also I pray for my friends. Today I remember and ask your blessing for . . .

As Jesus prayed for his enemies, so I pray for those who cause me pain and difficulty. May the tangled relationships be unraveled, and the wounds healed, and through the mystery of your grace may we become friends. I pray for . . .

I pray for . . .

Thanksgiving

I will worship the Lord with gladness and come into God's presence with singing. I will come to God's house with thanksgiving. For the Lord is good; his steadfast love endures forever.[4]

I give thanks to God for . . .

Dedication

This little light of mine, I'm goin'a let it shine.
Everywhere I go, I goin'a let it shine,
Let it shine, let it shine, let it shine.[5]

Silence

BENEDICTION

The grace of the Lord Jesus Christ, the love of God, and the communion of the Holy Spirit be with you. Amen.

NOTES ON CHAPTER 1

CREDITS FOR PRAYER GUIDE ONE

1. Psalm 46:10.
2. From an African-American spiritual.
3. Psalm 63:1–5 (TEV).
4. Adapted from Psalm 100.
5. From an African-American spiritual.

THINKING ABOUT GOD ⟨2⟩

*O*ne of the greatest problems many people have with prayer is their image of the One to whom their prayer is directed. Without a clear conception of what God is like, where God is to be found, and how God relates to the world, we are likely to be hesitant and limited in prayer. So the starting place for a discussion of thinking about prayer can very reasonably be some reflection on how we can think about God.

OUR CONCEPTS OF GOD CAN ALWAYS GROW

*S*ome years ago in the San Francisco *Chronicle* Sunday paper, the "Question Man" column featured children from three to six years of age who had been asked, "What does God look like?" One six-year-old said, "God wears a nightgown and shoes like you wear at the beach and He's tall. He lives up in heaven. He can see everybody but nobody sees him because He's spirit. He's real nice. He does things for people and makes things, too. Things like trees. He never goes to sleep because at night everybody's asking Him to watch so they'll be all right."

Another six-year-old said: "Jesus and God have this circle over their heads and they always try to walk careful so they stay right underneath it. It lights up. Jesus and God live up in

Heaven. Sometimes God comes here but He stays up high. In church He stays way in the top part."

And a four-year-old said: "Sometimes you can kind of see God when you look way up at the trees. You can kind of see a face. It looks like a face. Maybe it's Him."

Adults, confronted by the "Question Man," might not be quite as imaginative as the children, but they would certainly give a wide variety of answers. God, for some, is a man with white hair and a beard—much like Michelangelo's picture of God painted on the ceiling of the Sistine Chapel in the Vatican. For others, God looks like the pictures of Jesus they have seen in their churches. For some, feminine qualities are included in their image of God. God may be imaged as far away, or as close at hand. God may be envisioned as loving and merciful, or as righteously angry and frightening.

How God is imaged, how one thinks of God relating to the world, will powerfully impact how one prays. Some images of God make prayer come naturally and easily. Other images of God limit prayer or make it very difficult to pray with any sense of satisfaction.

Fortunately, it is possible for us to grow in our understanding of God, even as we grow in our understanding of prayer. In fact, the pilgrimage of faith is an adventure in growing in our understanding of who and where God is, and what God is like.

Howard Thurman, the late dean of the chapel and professor at Boston University, had the practice of writing down in his journal at the beginning of each year a description of his understanding of the nature of God. At the beginning of the next year, he read what he had written the previous year. As he wrote his new description, he said, he felt that if he had not grown in his perception of God, he would consider the year just ending as a year of wasted time.

GETTING TO KNOW YOU

Growing in our understanding of who God is can be compared to our experience in getting to know another human being. There are some important similarities between these two experiences, but this is a limited and potentially misleading analogy. There are important differences as well. We will start with the similarities and later note the limits to the analogy.

What you think about another person and who the other person is are never exactly the same. We are never able to perceive everything that another person is. No one can ever know us just as we are. We may think that we know or understand another person well. But people who have lived together for more than fifty years acknowledge that there is always an element of surprise in the relationship, always something more to be learned about the other.

The mystery of the otherness that can never be known is even more true in our relationship with God. The being of God is beyond our comprehension. We can think many things about God, but our thoughts can never encompass all of his nature and being.

One of the classics of Christian spirituality describes God as hidden completely from our view by a "cloud of unknowing." The anonymous fourteenth-century writer says that God's being is so much beyond our comprehension that our human language can never express that being. Even our thoughts cannot come near to what God is.

In the Book of Exodus there are two stories about attempts made by Moses to comprehend who God is. In the third chapter, he asked for God's name. In the Hebrew culture, this was a way to ask for the key to God's identity. The answer Moses received is "I am who I am" (Exod. 3:14). In the thirty-third chapter, Moses asked to see God's glory. He was permitted only a partial vision, and he was told that no one can see God and live (Exod. 33:18–20). God remains beyond our comprehension. There is always mystery, always more to be known.

A second similarity between our knowing of another person and our knowing of God is that our concepts of the other in both cases can change and grow. The first time I encounter another person, I may be scarcely aware of her or him at all. Those of us who live in larger towns and cities are exposed to many people whose presence we virtually ignore. We have no concept of other drivers on the highway, strangers in a crowd at a ballgame, and sometimes even our neighbors down the street. If we do notice these people, we perceive superficial data such as age, gender, and race.

If we are willing to commit time and energy to the process, and if the other person is willing to be known, it is possible to expand this initial perception. The middle-aged man who delivers our mail each day may be discovered to be an affectionate and indulgent father to two lively teenagers, a season-ticket holder for the local baseball team, a whiz at growing tomatoes, and much more.

The scriptures record that our ancestors in faith grew in their understanding of God over a period of more than a thousand years. The changes in their image of how God was present with them are particularly interesting as we think about how God is present with us.

As the Hebrews came out of slavery in Egypt into the wilderness, they perceived God's presence in a pillar of cloud by day and a pillar of fire by night. After the debacle at Mount Sinai with the golden calf, God sent an angel to be their constant guide. But Moses established a Tent of Meeting where the people could meet with God in time of need. When Moses entered the tent, the pillar of cloud would come down and settle at the door of that tent (Exod. 33:7-9). Later the presence of God came to be associated with a box or ark which contained objects of religious value. In the story of King David, the people, finally settled in their new land, considered building a permanent house for the ark, for God's presence (2 Sam. 7:1–27).

Here an interesting transition takes place in the thinking of the people. God did not want a house of wood. God would create a "house" in the form of a dynasty—the House of David. God's presence would be carried through the dynasty, and the Messiah would come from the House of David, since God was present in a special way in David's descendants.

In the New Testament, still another transition in thinking about God takes place. Now God is present in Christ. "In Christ God was reconciling the world" (2 Cor. 5:19). "The Word became flesh and lived among us . . . full of grace and truth; we have seen his glory" (John 1:14).

Later God's presence came into the church in the Holy Spirit. According to Paul in his letters, the Spirit dwells in the Christian person (see Rom. 8:9; 1 Cor. 3:16; Eph. 5:18).

J. B. Phillips wrote a once-popular book entitled *Your God Is Too Small*, calling people to let their understanding of God grow. The "God-Is-Dead" movement of the 1960s heralded not the death of God, but the death of some old ideas of God that needed to be discarded so people's concepts of God could grow.

HOW WE GROW IN OUR CONCEPT OF GOD

*W*e grow in our concept of God in ways similar to the way we grow to know each other. For example, if I have just become acquainted with you, there are several ways that I could get to know you. One of these ways is by experiencing how you relate to me. If you listen carefully to what I say, hear the feelings behind my words, and let me know that you hear and care, I will come to think of you as a kind and sensitive person.

The Hebrew people came to think of God as the One who led them out of slavery. Repeatedly in the Hebrew scriptures, God is introduced as the one who led the people out of Egypt. Who God is was partially defined in terms of what God did— the way the people experienced God.

We grow in our perception of God by how we experience God relating to us. Some of our hymns report on these experiences.

Henry Van Dyke's poetry is set to music from Beethoven's Ninth Symphony: "Thou art giving and forgiving, ever blessing, ever blest, well-spring of the joy of living, ocean depth of happy rest."

Juan Luis Garcia makes Psalm 33 contemporary with his hymn on the righteousness and justice of God:

> "Righteous and just is the word of our Lord; faithful and marvelous are the Lord's works. Justice and right are what God loves, they sit on thrones at God's right hand. And from the Lord's lovingkindness all the earth is filled with mercy."

C. Eric Lincoln, in a contemporary hymn of praise, says:

> How like a gentle spirit deep within
> God reins our fervent passions day by day,
> And gives us strength to challenge and to win
> Despite the perils of our chosen way. . . .
> Through all our fretful claims of sex and race
> The universal love of God shines through,
> For God is love transcending style and place
> And all the idle options we pursue.

We also speak about our experiences with God in familiar liturgies like the Korean Creed.

> We believe in the one God,
> creator and sustainer of all things . . .
> the source of all goodness and beauty, all truth and love.
> We believe in Jesus Christ, God manifest in the flesh,
> our teacher, example, and Redeemer, the Savior of the world.
> We believe in the Holy Spirit,
> God present with us for guidance, for comfort,
> and for strength.

If we have experienced God as a comforting presence in a time of pain or sorrow or loneliness, then we can think of God as one who is close to us and who cares about us. If we have had a mystical "oceanic experience" of the oneness of all creation, then we can think of God as the one in whom the whole of creation has unity. If we have experienced the life and teachings of Jesus as guiding our value formation, then we can think of God in Christ as the way and the truth and the life.

A second way I can come to know you better is through what others tell me about their experiences with you. In our scriptures and traditions, we have the record of centuries of people's experience with God. The sum of the testimony in our Judeo-Christian heritage is a resource of incredible richness, adequate for more than a lifetime of firsthand experience.

A third way in which I can come to a fuller, clearer concept of who you are is indirect. It may be that if I am really to see you, my perceptions of the nature of reality will have to change. James Clavell, in his novels, *Tai-Pan* and *Shogun*, depicts Europeans making their first contacts with the people of China and Japan. These early adventurers thought of the Asians as uncivilized barbarians. In fact, Asian habits of personal hygiene and systems of community organization were in many ways more civilized than those of the Europeans. A knowledge of the long history and rich culture of these newly discovered people would have given them a different perception of their new acquaintances.

As our perceptions of the reality of our universe expand, our concept of God can grow as well. In a world of space travel, it is not easy to think of God as "up there in the sky." New understandings of the nature of reality coming to us through scientific research are not a threat to the existence of God, but an invitation to us to stretch our thoughts about God.

The best way for me to get to know you is if you choose to reveal yourself to me. If you decide that you would like for me to know you, and you decide to tell me about yourself, to show me who you are, then I have my best chance for growing in my concept of you. Christians believe this is what God has done in Jesus Christ.

God has come to be with us in Christ as a way of responding to the age-old request expressed by Moses, "Let us see your glory" (Exod. 33:18, author's paraphrase). Christ is sometimes referred to as our "window on divinity," for in Christ we are able to see into the nature of God. For Christians, Christ is the supreme revelation. If we want to grow in our ways of thinking about God, we can pay attention to what God has chosen to share with us in Christ.

Further, it is the testimony of Christians that this revelation continues through the presence with us of the spirit of the risen Christ or the Holy Spirit. God's self-revelation was not just a one-time event.

One final use of this limited analogy may be appropriate to our purposes here. We do not need to wait until we get to know someone completely before we establish a relationship with that person. In fact, if we do not establish some kind of relationship, the chances of getting to know this person in a significant way are slim. If you and I meet, it is possible for me to begin to communicate with you on the basis of very limited information. Then my relationship with you and my concept of you can grow together.

It is possible to worship God through adoration before we have our concepts of God all worked out. It is possible to share our concerns and to listen for the word of God without having our images crystal clear. It is possible to have a significant prayer relationship with God, even to love him, without knowing everything about his nature.

Thinking about God is a dynamic process with endless possibilities for growth. Prayer is one of the ways in which we open ourselves to a relationship with God in which our concept of God and our friendship with God can grow.

PREPARATION AND CENTERING

God is present in the world today, making new the whole creation. I will rejoice and be glad in this day![6]

PRAISE AND ADORATION

All thy works with joy surround thee,
Earth and heaven reflect thy rays,
Stars and angels sing around thee,
Center of unbroken praise.
Field and forest, vale and mountain,
Flowery meadow, flashing sea,
Chanting bird and flowing fountain,
Call us to rejoice in thee.[7]

I praise you for . . .

CONFESSION

Almighty God, to you all hearts are open, all desires known, and from you no secrets are hidden. Cleanse the thoughts of my heart by the inspiration of your Holy Spirit, that I may perfectly love you and worthily magnify your holy name, through Christ our Lord. Amen.[8]

I confess that the thoughts of my heart need to be
cleansed today in these ways . . .

If we confess our sins,
God is faithful and just,

and will forgive our sins
and cleanse us from all unrighteousness.[9]

MEDITATIVE READING OF SCRIPTURE

(Passages about growth in the concept of God's nature)

Day One:	Exodus 3:13–15
Day Two:	Exodus 33:12–23
Day Three:	2 Samuel 7:1–27
Day Four:	2 Corinthians 5:16–21
Day Five:	Romans 8:9–11
Day Six:	1 Corinthians 3:16–17
Day Seven:	Ephesians 5:15–20

Insights from the scriptures:

PETITIONS

I pray for spiritual growth. As I grow in prayer, may I see you more clearly, love you more dearly, and follow you more nearly.[10]

With Moses, I pray that you will show me your glory. Lift my vision from the temporary to the eternal . . .

I bring to you the deepest needs of my life, as I understand them, asking for gifts of your grace in response to them . . .

I pray for . . .

INTERCESSIONS

I pray for my community, that good may triumph over evil, that love may conquer hate. I pray especially for this need in my community . . .

I pray for my church and its leaders, that they may be faithful to the gospel and effective in mission . . . I pray especially for . . .

I pray for my family, especially for this person with special need . . .

I pray for . . .

THANKSGIVING

It is good to give thanks to the Lord,
    to sing praises to your name, O Most High;
to declare your steadfast love in the morning,
    and your faithfulness by night.
For you, O Lord, have made me glad by your work;
    at the works of your hands I sing for joy. [11]

I give thanks to you for . . .

DEDICATION

O Lord, with your eyes you have searched me,
And while smiling, have spoken my name.
Now my boats left on the shoreline behind me,
By your side I will seek other seas. [12]

SILENCE

BENEDICTION

May the power and presence of Jesus Christ give you strength and wisdom as you go. Amen.

CREDITS FOR PRAYER GUIDE TWO

6. Psalm 118:24 (author's paraphrase).

7. From the hymn "Joyful, Joyful, We Adore Thee." Words by Henry Van Dyke.

8. Adapted from "A Service of Word and Table I" in *The United Methodist Hymnal.*

9. From "Prayers of Confession, Assurance, and Pardon" in *The United Methodist Hymnal.*

10. Richard of Chichester.

11. Psalm 92:1–2, 4.

12. From the hymn "Lord, You Have Come to the Lakeshore." Words by Cesareo Gabrain.

GOD AS MORE THAN PERSONAL SPIRIT 3

*T*hinking about God can be compared to thinking about another person. But thinking about God is also different from thinking about another person in some very important ways.

It is easy for us to think about God as a person because so much of biblical imagery is personal. God walks in the Garden of Eden, bargains with Abraham, gets angry at Mount Sinai, talks to the prophets. It is easy to understand how Michelangelo could paint God on the ceiling of the Sistine Chapel as an old man with a white beard. There is something in all of us that needs to think of God as personal. "Personal" easily becomes "person."

If God is a person, then the next logical step is to create God in our own image with a physical body. The masculine image of God's body is the product of the patriarchal society in which our faith has taken root and grown. A deity is usually identified with that which is most highly valued in a society. In some cultures, the god is female; in some it is an animal or tree or mountain. Our patriarchal ancestors saw God as a human-like male. The long white beard is probably the product of the ancient association of wisdom with age.

But God is spirit. "God is spirit, and those who worship him must worship in spirit and truth," John reports Jesus as saying to the Samaritan woman (John 4:24). The writer of the first letter to Timothy speaks of God as "immortal, invisible" (1 Tim. 1:17). This text has been set to music in one of the great hymns of the church by Walter Chalmers Smith, "Immortal, invisible, God only wise, In light inaccessible hid from our eyes."

Thinking of God as spirit is not so difficult if we refer once again to the analogy of human relationships. When I relate to you, I relate to more than your body. We communicate through our bodies, our voices and ears, our movements and eyes, our sense of touch. But the kindness and sensitivity that I have come to know are expressions of your spirit. There is, however, a difference between our finite human spirit and the eternal divine Spirit. God is not just a larger disembodied version of our human spirit. God is not confined to the possibilities of personality.

Another way of saying the same things is to affirm that God is more than personal. This means that God is at least personal, for God is able to communicate with the personal dimension of creation and to be involved in personal relationships. God is not impersonal. God can be addressed as a "Thou," a personal being. Because we know only two kinds of personal beings, male and female, and the English language only provides for conversation about "he's" and" she's," we get caught in the trap of referring to God as "he." But God's being transcends sexuality.

God is spirit, and God is more than personal. Getting our minds around what it means to be more-than-personal divine spirit may be the toughest part of the process of thinking about God.

What more is it possible for us to think? For our faith to be healthy and effective, our perceptions of God must fit with our general experience of reality. They must be consistent with what we know about how the universe functions. To be Christian, our concept of God must be also scriptural. Poised as we are in history with a mature Christian tradition and a two-hundred-year-old scientific revolution, what can we say about the nature of God that is both reasonable and Christian?

It is both Christian and reasonable to think of God as present with us in every moment. Primitive images of God have usually located God "out there" somewhere. "Out there" is often also "up there" in heaven. Much of our religious language projects this sense of distance between ourselves and God. Certainly God may be thought of as beyond us—up there and out there. But God can also be thought of as with us and within us.

Jean-Pierre De Caussade, a French Jesuit teacher and writer in the eighteenth century, used the phrase "the sacrament of the present moment." That is where God can be found, he said. De Caussade also wrote, "Faith sees that Jesus Christ lives in everything and works through all history to the end of time, that every fraction of a second, every atom of matter, contains a fragment of his hidden life and his secret activity." Later he added that "God's action penetrates every atom of your body, into the very marrow of your bones."

Dame Julian of Norwich, an English mystic from the fourteenth century, became aware of this absolute presence of God. She is quoted as saying, "Then our Lord opened my spiritual eyes and showed me the soul in the middle of my heart. . . . Nor will he quit the place he holds in our soul forever—as I see it. For in us is he completely at home, and has his eternal dwelling."

The implications of this way of thinking about God are important for the way we think about prayer, especially for those who have groped around for God outside themselves somewhere. Offering spiritual advice to Madame Guyon, a Franciscan friar said, "Madame, you are seeking without that which you have within. Accustom yourself to seek God in your own heart and you will find him."

Samuel Longfellow wrote a hymn that expresses the church's faith in this absolute nearness of God.

> God of the earth, the sky, the sea,
> Maker of all above, below;
> Creation lives and moves in thee,
> Thy present life through all doth flow.
>
> Thy love is in the sunshine's glow,
> Thy life is in the quickening air;
> When lightnings flash and storm winds blow,
> There is thy power; thy law is there.
>
> We feel thy calm at evening's hour,
> Thy grandeur in the march of night,
> And when the morning breaks in power,
> We hear thy word, "Let there be light!"
>
> But higher far and far more clear,
> Thee in (our) spirit we behold;
> Thine image and thyself are there,
> Th' indwelling God, proclaimed of old.

It follows naturally to think of the God who is present in every moment in our inner being as knowing every detail of our lives. The psalmist gives poetic expression to this experience of God:

> O Lord, you have searched me and known me.
> You know when I sit down and when I rise up;
>> you discern my thoughts from far away.
> You search out my path and my lying down,
>> and are acquainted with all my ways.
> Even before a word is on my tongue,
>> O Lord, you know it completely.
> You hem me in, behind and before,
>> and lay your hand upon me,
> Such knowledge is too wonderful for me;
>> it is so high that I cannot attain it.
>
> Where can I go from your spirit?
>> Or where can I flee from your presence?
> If I ascend to heaven, you are there;
>> if I make my bed in Sheol, you are there.
> If I take the wings of the morning
>> and settle at the farthest limits of the sea,
> even there your hand shall lead me,
>> and your right hand shall hold me fast.
> If I say, "Surely the darkness shall cover me,
>> and the light around me become night,"
> even the darkness is not dark to you;
>> the night is as bright as the day,
>> for darkness is as light to you.
>
> For it was you who formed my inward parts;
>> you knit me together in my mother's womb.
> I praise you, for I am fearfully and wonderfully made.
>> Wonderful are your works; that I know very well.

My frame was not hidden from you,
> when I was being made in secret,
> intricately woven in the depths of the earth.
Your eyes beheld my unformed substance.
In your book were written all the days that were formed for
> me when none of them as yet existed.
How weighty to me are your thoughts, O God!
> How vast is the sum of them!
I try to count them—they are more than the sand;
> I come to the end—I am still with you.

— Psalm 139:1–18

In the story of the selection of David as King, the Lord says to Samuel, "The Lord does not see as mortals see; they look on the outward appearance, but the Lord looks on the heart" (1 Sam. 16:7).

One image of God that makes prayer difficult is the "top-level executive" image. It is not surprising that in a world of giant bureaucracies and multinational corporations, this kind of imagery should be a problem. We see top executives making only major decisions, surrounded by busy staffs who handle the details and the less important decisions. We hear that to make it to the top you have to know how to delegate. It is easy for that kind of hierarchical thinking to be transposed into our thinking about God.

Such a God, of course, could not be bothered with us—unless, perhaps, we were desperate. We should only pray to such a God about the major problems of the world—wars, droughts, hunger, injustice. Certainly there is no place for the ordinary cares and details of our lives. Such an image of God comes from our human experience with each other; it has no basis in the scriptural resources of our faith.

The early church remembered Jesus saying, "Your father knows what you need before you ask him" (Matt. 6:8). God knows us even better than we know ourselves. "Even the hairs of your head are all counted" (Matt. 10:30).

The God whose creative power has made possible the whole universe is present with us, in us, in every split second of our existence, knowing us behind all of our self-doubts, masks, and pretensions, knowing us more honestly and intimately than we know ourselves.

Truth can only be completely perceived from the perspective of God. You cannot know me completely. Even I do not really know myself. Only God knows the full reality of who I am. The same is true about the condition of the world at any time. There is important religious insight in the old cliché, "Only God knows!"

This Spirit which is so near to us and knows us so well is beyond us and beyond all of creation. The word "transcend" is an important word in the Christian tradition of thinking about God. It communicates that the God who dwells in the creation also exists beyond the creation. God is in the world, but the world does not contain all of God.

Oliver Wendell Holmes captures his vision of the combination of the greatness and the nearness of God in a hymn:

> Lord of all being, throned afar,
> Thy glory flames from sun and star;
> Center and soul of every sphere,
> Yet to each loving heart how near!

Sometimes in worship Christians become so conscious of God's nearness that they develop a kind of cozy, "chummy" way of relating to God that does not seem to take into account God's transcendence. This image of God almost resembles the ancient gods who were thought to belong to one particular tribe and to protect the interests of their little group. God is not our private possession, but is the God of all creation. In *Reality and Prayer*, John Magee points out:

> We are led by Jesus to dare to call God "Father" in an intimate colloquy of the soul.... Yet we entirely miss the meaning of this intimate communion unless it is set against the awesome vastness of the Adorable Majesty ... The intimate and the ultimate ... are qualities that mutually enrich each other. Only in the wedding of these polar truths is the mystery of God's gracious presence saved from stupid sentimentality. This does not mean that we are to be less intimate, but rather that we are to know this intimacy against the background of ultimacy.

It is both Christian and reasonable to say that it is in God that we experience our unity with the whole of creation. God is present in every moment to every part of the whole universe. In that co-presence we have our oneness with each other. The universal nature of God is clearly expressed in John Oxenham's hymn:

> In Christ there is no east or west,
> In him no south or north;
> But one great fellowship of love
> Throughout the whole wide earth.
>
> In Christ shall true hearts everywhere
> Their high communion find;

His service is the golden cord
Close binding humankind.

Marshall McLuhan coined the phrase "the global village," giving us a new way to refer to our increasingly close-knit world community. Space explorations have given us photographs of the earth and a new perception of our common destiny as a human race. But our common life is not a simple matter of physical proximity and interdependence. We are one with each other because of our common relationship to God. Paul Tillich describes God as "the ground of being."

In *Science and the Modern World*, Alfred North Whitehead speaks of our existence in the universe as a matter of "through and through togetherness." He says that God is "the binding element in the world." In God, everything is interrelated with everything else.

When we pray, we are in communication with one who is more than personal spirit.

PREPARATION AND CENTERING

I'm goin'a pray when the Spirit says pray, and obey the Spirit of the Lord.[13]

Those who wait for the Lord shall renew their strength, they shall mount up with wings like eagles, they shall run and not be weary, they shall walk and not faint.[14]

PRAISE AND ADORATION

O for a thousand tongues to sing
　　my great Redeemer's praise,
the glories of my God and King,
　　the triumphs of his grace.
Jesus! the name that charms our fears,
　　that bids our sorrow cease;
'tis music to the sinner's ears,
　　'tis life and health and peace.[15]

I praise you for . . .

CONFESSION

If we say that we have no sin, we deceive ourselves, and the truth is not in us. If we confess our sins, he who is faithful and just will forgive us our sins and cleanse us from all unrighteousness.[16]

I confess . . .

Forgive me and purify me and guide me into life eternal.

MEDITATIVE READING OF SCRIPTURE

Day One: 1 Timothy 1:12–17
Day Two: Psalm 139:1–12
Day Three: Psalm 139:13–18
Day Four: Matthew 6:5–8
Day Five: Matthew 10:26–31
Day Six: John 4:7–15
Day Seven: John 4:16–24

Insights from the scriptures:

PETITIONS

I pray for strength in my inner being as I confront this challenging part of my life . . .

I pray for freedom from fear and anxiety. Help me to find peace. Help me to know what to do about the things that frighten me, especially . . .

I pray for living water to satisfy the thirst that nothing else can quench . . .

I pray for . . .

INTERCESSIONS

I pray for the victims of violence. Help us to destroy the roots of violence among us, and to build a future of order with justice, respect for human life and peace. I pray for . . .

I pray for the poor, the hungry and the homeless. May they be remembered and their needs met out of your bounty as we learn to save and share . . .

I pray for the church, that it may be a faithful representative of Christ in the world . . .

I pray for those who have asked me to pray for them . . .

I pray for . . .

THANKSGIVING

Gracious God, I am thankful for all your goodness to me and to all of your creation. I thank you for creating, preserving and blessing my life. I thank you for the gift of salvation in Jesus Christ, for the ways in which you continue to sustain and guide me in every day, and for the hope you make possible. Make me so aware of your gifts that I may respond not only with my lips in praise and thanksgiving, but with my life in holy living and dedicated service to you.[17]

I thank you for . . .

DEDICATION

Send me, Lord. Lead me, Lord, Fill me Lord. Send me, Lord.

SILENCE

BENEDICTION

May Christ live in you and shine through you as light for the world. Amen.

CREDITS FOR PRAYER GUIDE THREE

13. From an African-American spiritual.

14. Isaiah 40:31.

15. From the hymn "O for a Thousand Tongues to Sing." Words by Charles Wesley.

16. 1 John 1:8–9.

17. Adapted from *The Book of Common Prayer*.

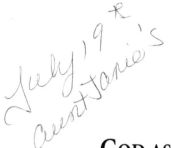

GOD AS CREATIVE/ RESPONSIVE LOVE 4

The Christian understanding of the nature of God as revealed to us in Christ has been summed up in three words, "God is Love" (1 John 4:8). The one with whom we communicate in prayer is one whose nature is love. The Psalms, the hymnbook of the Old Testament, sing God's praises for "steadfast love" which is abundant (Psalm 69:13), "good" (Psalm 69:16), "higher than the heavens" (Psalm 108:4), and which "endures forever" (Psalm 107:1). The New Testament identifies the coming of Christ as the gift of God's love.

> For God so loved the world that he gave his only Son, so that everyone who believes in him may not perish but may have eternal life. Indeed, God did not send the Son into the world to condemn the world, but in order that the world might be saved through him.
>
> — John 3:16–17

God's love is not just the sentimental affection that is sometimes associated with the word love. The biblical picture of divine love is of action on behalf of the beloved, not just positive feelings. God's love is expressed in God's care for the whole creation.

In the Old Testament, God's nature is summed up in the word "righteousness." But that righteousness expressed itself as love. The law was understood to have been given to the people of God as an expression of God's care for the people. The law regulated and protected relationships in the community in ways intended to provide order with justice. The final intent of the law was to create a healthy social environment in which human life could flourish.

Jesus expanded this Hebrew understanding of God's love by repeatedly addressing God as Father. God, says Jesus, cares for the creation, clothing the grass and feeding the ravens, and providing for the human creatures as well (Luke 12:22-31). Jesus revealed this love in his life of concern and care for others. The depth of this love is made known in the cross.

Paul declared that "God's love has been poured into our hearts through the Holy Spirit that has been given to us" (Rom. 5:5). And he makes one of the great affirmations of Christian faith in this love in his letter to the Romans:

> For I am convinced that neither death, nor life, nor angels, nor rulers, nor things present, nor things to come, nor powers, nor height, nor depth, nor anything else in all creation will be able to separate us from the love of God in Christ Jesus our Lord.
>
> — Romans 8:38–39

In their book *Process Theology: An Introductory Exposition*, John Cobb and David Griffin point out that God's love can be thought of in two ways: as creative love and as responsive love. In fact, all of the ways God is experienced in the Christian tradition can be understood as an expression of creative-responsive love.

As creative love, God calls the world to realize the ideal possibilities which are God's will for the world. Jean-Pierre

De Caussade speaks of "God's treasury," which is unlocked by faith. In God's treasury are all the possibilities for the maximum well-being of the creation. A variety of words are used to describe what God wills for us: shalom, strength of beauty, peace, complete fulfillment, the kingdom of God.

God is not a great cosmic Santa Claus to whom we come with a list or the great "vending machine in the sky" with handles for all the goodies we might want. But God does desire that we realize the potential of each moment of our existence. God calls us forward into a future of possibility. God confronts us in every moment with our possibilities and potential. When we pray, we connect with the one who would communicate these possibilities to us.

Alfred North Whitehead, writing in *Process and Reality*, describes God as "the poet of the world, with tender patience leading it by his vision of truth, beauty and goodness." God goes before us with the ideal possibilities for us, seeking to lure us on.

The decisions we have made in the past determine our starting place in creating the present. But the past does not determine completely what our present is or what our future shall be. God is actively present with us, presenting us with new possibilities for our unique place in life. We are free to respond to God's "call forward." We cannot escape our past or change it, but we do not have to be captives of the past. Because of God's activity in us and among us, there is hope.

In a hymn based on Psalm 8, Curtis Beach describes his sense of being called into the future by God's creative love envisioning possibilities for us:

> O how wondrous, O how glorious
> Is thy name in every land!

Thou whose purpose moves before us
Toward the goal that thou has planned.

'Tis thy will our hearts are seeking,
Conscious of our human need.
Spirit in our spirit speaking,
Make us thine, O God, indeed!

The power which God uses in calling us forward is the power of persuasion or attraction. Power is sometimes exercised by pushing, forcing, altering by fiat. Power is sometimes exercised by attraction, influence, like a magnet. In the hymn "Sing Praise to God Who Reigns Above," Johann Schutz wrote, "As with a mother's tender Hand, (God) leads his own, his chosen band." This is the kind of power we witness in the life of Christ who came humbly, lived without the signs and symbols of coercive power, resisted in the desert the temptation to seek the power of force, and yet had tremendous power to attract and to call forth the best in people. In the face of the dominating, brute force of the Roman Empire and the Jewish religious establishment, he suffered the crucifixion. Yet the force of love that dwelt in Christ has ultimately prevailed. God works in the world through the persuasive power of love.

The church sings its faith in God's call forward. With the hymnist William Williams, we sing, "Guide me, O thou great Jehovah, pilgrim through this barren land." And in Joseph Gilmore's words, "He leadeth me, he leadeth me, by his own hand he leadeth me."

God may be experienced not only as creative love, but also as responsive love. We do not take advantage of all of the possibilities that God offers to us. In each moment, we have not only the influence of the past and the call of God into the future. We have our own free will. What we become is the result of what we choose to do with what we are given. We make mistakes. We fail. We choose destructive rather than constructive patterns of behavior. Sometimes we get ourselves into trouble. Sometimes forces and factors beyond our control cause us pain and suffering. Things don't go smoothly, accidents occur, disease develops, life gets complicated. But God is present with us in all these circumstances as responsive love.

> O Love divine that stooped to share
> Our sharpest pang, our bitterest tear,
> On thee we cast each earthborn care;
> We smile at pain while thou art near.
> — Oliver Wendell Holmes

One image of God that blocks prayer is the stern judge or divine criticizing parent, waiting to catch us in disobedience in order to punish. Such images may originate in childhood, when we hear threats that God will punish us if we misbehave. Such images lurking in the back of an adult mind need to be cast out before prayer can become a positive opportunity.

One of the most beautiful pictures of the nature of God is given in the parable of the prodigal son. A central figure in the parable is the forgiving father, who runs to welcome the child who has wasted all he was given. The father calls for an extravagant celebration because the prodigal has seen the errors of his ways and has come back to the relationship of the family. The father bestows on his son new gifts of grace. God's love is expressed in forgiveness, which is offered in the face of our rejection of God and our wandering ways.

God's offer of forgiveness is one of the central affirmations of the Christian faith. The scriptures testify to it:

> The Lord is merciful and gracious,
>> slow to anger and abounding in steadfast love.
> He will not always accuse,
>> nor will he keep his anger forever.
> He does not deal with us according to our sins,
>> nor repay us according to our iniquities.
> For as the heavens are high above the earth,
>> so great is his steadfast love toward those who fear him;
>>> as far as the east is from the west,
>> so far he removes our transgressions from us.
> As a father has compassion for his children,
>> so the Lord has compassion for those who fear him,
> For he knows how we were made;
>> he remembers that we are dust.
>
> — Psalm 103:8–14

The great creeds of the church witness to this truth. In the Apostles' Creed, we say, "I believe in . . . the forgiveness of sins." The church sings its faith in forgiveness. In Charles Wesley's moving hymn, "O for a Thousand Tongues to Sing," we are assured that "he breaks the power of canceled sin, he sets the prisoner free."

God's forgiveness can be experienced in two ways. God accepts us just as we are and offers new possibilities appropriate to where we are. No matter what we have done or have omitted doing, God is still with us, leading us with creative love. We are "justified" by God in the sense that God will give us only what we can or will accept. Those who are responsive to God are able to receive increasingly rich challenges, while those who are unresponsive have fewer opportunities. But wherever we are, God is there with us.

God's forgiveness can also be experienced in what God does with our past. The past cannot be erased. But God takes the past into the divine being. The good, the bad, and the indifferent experiences of the world are taken into God's own being as they become part of the past. There all of the values are synthesized and preserved.

God's forgiveness might be compared to the skill of an experienced weaver. When the weaver makes a mistake in working with the fabric, he incorporates the mistake into the design and continues his creative work. Even though we as humans are flawed by sin, God continues to work with us through his forgiveness to make us into beings who reflect his love and grace.

Our failure and sin are not without cost to God. The cross of Christ, the central symbol of Christianity, is a symbol of God's suffering for our sin. God has suffered, and God continues to suffer for and with us.

God is affected by what we do. This may be a shocking idea for some people. Our ways of thinking about God have been influenced by Greek philosophy as well as by the scriptures. The idea that God is unchangeable has come into our heritage from Greek philosophy as well as by the scriptures. The God of responsive love is a God who is affected by what we do.

In the Old Testament we find the account of Abraham bargaining with God to save the city of Sodom. God wanted to destroy the city because of its extreme evil. Abraham convinced God to spare Sodom temporarily for the sake of the righteous people who lived there (Gen. 18:20-33). God's mind was also changed about destroying Nineveh (Jonah 3:10). It is both reasonable and Christian to believe that God is affected by us and by our prayers.

This responsive love of God provides the ground of meaning for our existence. Our simplest actions, our most private thoughts can matter to us because they matter to God. They make an everlasting contribution to the world as preserved in God. No matter what happens in the future, even if our accomplishments seem to add up to nothing, our lives are meaningful because what we do matters to God. This includes our prayers.

Our concepts of God fall short of the reality of God. All of our language about God is necessarily symbolic. We can speak of God as father, as mother, as the ground of being, as the fellow-sufferer who understands, as the one who calls. But these are metaphors. If we make idols of any of our metaphors, we lock ourselves into one stage of spiritual growth. Assuming that we know more than we do may be necessary in the life of faith. But assuming that we have perfect understanding of God can choke and smother our growth in the life of the spirit.

Our pilgrimage of faith involves a dynamic relationship with God in which our limited and inadequate metaphors are in the process of being replaced by images that penetrate more deeply into the reality of God. The worship of God is an adventure in discovery and understanding.

Preparation and Centering

Send your light and your truth, O God; may they lead me to you.[18]

Praise and Adoration

I sing the almighty power of God,
    that made the mountains rise;
that spread the flowing seas abroad,
    and built the lofty skies.
I sing the wisdom that ordained
    the sun to rule the day;
the moon shines full at God's command,
    and all the stars obey.

I sing the goodness of the Lord,
    who filled the earth with food,
who formed the creatures thru the Word,
    and then pronounced them good.
Lord, how thy wonders are displayed,
    where'er I turn my eye;
if I survey the ground I tread,
    or gaze upon the sky.[19]

I praise you for . . .

CONFESSION

Merciful God, I confess that I have not loved you with my whole heart. I have failed to be an obedient part of your church. I have not done your will, I have broken your law, I have rebelled against your love, I have not loved my neighbors, and I have not heard the cry of the needy. Forgive me, I pray. Free me for joyful obedience, through Jesus Christ my Lord. Amen.

I confess . . .

Hear the good news:
> Christ died for you while you were yet a sinner;
> > that proves God's love toward you.
> In the name of Jesus Christ, you are forgiven! [20]

MEDITATIVE READING OF SCRIPTURE

Day One:	Genesis 1:1–31
Day Two:	Psalm 8
Day Three:	Psalm 103:1–5
Day Four:	John 3:16–17
Day Five:	Luke 15:11–32
Day Six:	Psalm 103:6–18
Day Seven:	Romans 8:38–39

PETITIONS

I pray for the expansion of my love by the infusion of your love into my heart. Purge me of hatred, vengefulness, and prejudice with the power of your love. I pray for new resources for loving in this situation . . .

I pray for healing of my body, my mind, and my spirit. Help me to do my part in releasing the springs of health that you have placed in me . . .

Fill me with the knowledge of your will and with all the wisdom and understanding that your Spirit gives as I confront the problems and decisions of this day . . .

I pray for . . .

INTERCESSIONS

I pray for those in pain or distress. Grant to them courage, relief and refreshment, and the comfort of your sustaining presence. I remember especially . . .

I pray for those I find difficult to love. When I am worn out by them, irritated by their needs, impatient with their idiosyncrasies and limitations, give me grace to see below the surface into their hearts, to sympathize more deeply with their needs, to support what is lovely in them, and to know how to pray for them. I pray for . . .

I pray for those who grieve over loss. Protect them from bitterness and despair, and bring them through to peace and new hope. I remember especially . . .

I pray for . . .

THANKSGIVING

For the harvests of the Spirit, thanks be to God;
for the good we all inherit, thanks be to God;
for the wonders that astound us,
for the truths that still confound us,
most of all, that love has found us,
thanks be to God. [21]

I thank you for . . .

DEDICATION

Here I am, Lord, for you called me. Speak, Lord, for your
servant is listening. [22]

SILENCE

BENEDICTION

Glory to God whose power, working in us, can do infinitely
more than we can ask or imagine. Amen.

Notes on Chapter 4

CREDITS FOR PRAYER GUIDE FOUR

18. Adapted from Psalm 43:3.

19. From the hymn "I Sing the Almighty Power of God." Words by Isaac Watts.

20. Adapted from "A Service of Word and Table I" in *The United Methodist Hymnal.*

21. From the hymn "For the Fruits of This Creation." Words by Fred Pratt Green.

22. Adapted from 1 Samuel 3:8–10.

THINKING ABOUT PRAYER · 5

*P*rayer is a "mysterious linking of the human and the Divine . . . an incomprehensible wonder, a miracle of miracles," says Friedrich Heiler in his book *Prayer*. It is a living communion between human beings and God, the bringing of our finite spirits into direct touch with the infinite spirit of God in a conscious and intentional way. This linking is made possible by God's initiative, by the working of the Spirit within us.

In the last few years, we have experienced many marvelous developments in communication. We can talk directly to people all around the globe. The conversation flows back and forth almost as if we were in the same room. Human beings soar through space and carry on conversations with their colleagues on earth. We fax instantly what used to spend days in the mail. Mobile equipment makes us available for communication anywhere we go. Beepers, computer networks, satellites, and picture phones keep us in touch with one another in ways that people a hundred years ago would have found miraculous.

Our ancestors in faith have experienced communication between the human spirit and God's spirit for thousands of years. This "direct touch" has been taken for granted as far back in history as our biblical record goes. Yet it, too, remains a source of wonder and amazement. It is to this miracle of miracles that we attempt now to give some careful thought. Assuming what has already been said about God, how can we think about prayer?

PRAYER AS OPENNESS

A key word in thinking about prayer is openness. God is always present with us, relating to us in every moment of our lives as creative and responsive love. But we are free to choose either to ignore that presence or to give attention to it. Prayer is the act of being intentionally open to God.

We are bombarded by an incredible number of messages and bits of information in the course of a day. There is no way that we could be consciously and intentionally open to all of them. We have to screen out many of the signals that come to us through our senses of sight, hearing, smell, taste, and touch. We are not always free to choose what our environment will be, either internally or externally. But we do have some freedom of choice in deciding what our response to that environment will be.

If I am walking in a beautiful park on a warm, spring day, I can choose to listen for bird songs and look for birds. Or I can choose to enjoy the beauty of color in the new leaves and the flowers against the darker green of the grass and the blue of the sky. Or I can be absorbed in analyzing a painful disagreement with someone important to me and not be consciously aware of the birds or the colors at all.

Likewise, in a crowded restaurant, it is possible for me to keep up with a boring conversation at my table while listening in on a more interesting conversation at the next table! We do have the power to decide how we will divide our attention.

God is a constant part of our environment. We can ignore that presence, or we can open ourselves to communion with that presence. To open ourselves to God is to pray. Prayer involves two kinds of openness—openness to God and openness with God.

Some of the leaders of the Christian church in the second and third centuries used the Greek word *homilia* or its root form *homilein*, normally a reference to a form of preaching described as a familiar conversation, to refer to prayer. This word can mean being or living together, conversing or dealing with each other, encountering, being friends. Prayer is in some ways like a human social relationship or friendship. In friendship, we are open to the other person. We listen, respect, and try to understand the other person. We try to see things from her or his perspective. We are also open with a friend. We share ourselves honestly. We reveal what it is like to be who we are. We tell what is going on in our world. In prayer we are open to who God is and his truth and purposes. And we tell God who we are and what we need and desire.

Jesus gave his disciples a model for prayer that reflected this two-dimensional openness. In the Lord's Prayer, there are six major petitions. In the first three, attention is focused on God.

> Our Father in heaven,
>   hallowed be your name.
> Your kingdom come, your will be done,
>   on earth as it is in heaven
>   — Matthew 6:9–10

The one who prays is open to who God is, expresses respect for God's being, and shares in wanting what God wants for the world. The prayer begins with a response to God from the mind, the emotions, and the will of the one who prays. The second three petitions make known the requests of the disciples who pray:

> Give us this day our daily bread;
> And forgive us our debts as we also
> have forgiven our debtors;
> And do not bring us to the time of trial,
> but rescue us from the evil one.
> — Matthew 6:11–13

Our physical needs, our relationships, the struggles of our existence—the whole of our lives—are appropriately shared openly with God.

Perhaps our thinking about prayer can be helped by a more careful look at the two sides of our participation in this "mysterious linking" called prayer.

OPENNESS TO GOD

*P*rayer has been described as a time exposure of the soul to God. When film is exposed, it is changed. It reflects that to which it has been exposed. When we become open to God in prayer, we grant God the power to shape and transform us in the relationship. John Cobb speaks of the divine "field of force." When we open ourselves to God in prayer, we put ourselves in that field of force. Like metal filings in the force field of a powerful magnet, we will find ourselves attracted and creatively transformed. When we open ourselves to God, we give power to God's call forward to the vast possibilities that God offers to us.

A popular old gospel hymn by Annie S. Hawks expresses this openness to God:

> I need thee every hour
> Teach me thy will;
> And thy rich promises
> In me fulfill.

In *The Meaning of Prayer*, Harry Emerson Fosdick quotes Peter Annet, who pictures praying people as "like sailors who have cast anchor on a rock, and who imagine they are pulling the rock to themselves, when they are really pulling themselves to the rock." Christlikeness, or Christian maturity, is the goal toward which we will be drawn if we open ourselves to God in prayer. One of Samuel Longfellow's hymns invites this transformation.

> Holy Spirit, Truth divine,
> Dawn upon this soul of mine;
> Word of God and inward light,
> Wake my spirit, clear my sight.
>
> Holy Spirit, love divine,
> Glow within this heart of mine;
> Kindle every high desire;
> Perish self in thy pure fire.
>
> Holy Spirit, Power divine,
> Fill and nerve this will of mine;
> Grant that I may strongly live,
> Bravely bear, and nobly strive.

Holy Spirit, Right divine,
King within my conscience reign;
Be my Lord, and I shall be
Firmly bound, forever free.

When we open ourselves to God in prayer, we leave our private, enclosed worlds and enter a broader, shared world. We lift our eyes from our limited self-interest to look at reality from the perspective of God. Our inner world becomes connected to universality.

When we pray in openness to God, we make a way for the work of God's creative love in our lives. In "Opening" from *Diary of Daily Prayer*, J. Barrie Shepherd speaks of being open to God.

Lord, teach me to be open, and receptive in my praying.
So often, when I pray,
the only thing that is open is my mouth.
My eyes are shut tight,
and with them my mind and my heart.
Lord, teach me to be open to the leading of your Spirit
as I pray.

In these times of concern for dialog between persons,
I have allowed my praying to degenerate
into a tedious monolog
in which I do all the talking
and you do all the listening.
Yet it is written:
"Be still and know that I am God,"
And again:
"In quietness and in trust shall be your strength."

So teach me, Father,
that prayer is both a matter of speaking and of silence.
Draw especially close now
as I set a few minutes aside
to wait in silence,
and listen expectantly for your word:
your judgment on my sin,
your forgiveness in Jesus my Lord,
your response to my requests,
your call to my readiness.

Let me learn again, Lord,
the prayer of your servant, Samuel:
"Speak, Lord, for your servant hears."
And let me make this prayer my own
tonight and always.

OPENNESS WITH GOD

*H*arry Emerson Fosdick, in *The Meaning of Prayer*, points out that those who pray act on the faith that God cares personally for them. To pray actually puts our faith in God's love and care into practice.

The scriptures contain an abundance of models of honest, open self-revelation in prayer. In the time of restoration of the Hebrews after the exile, the prophet Ezra led his people in confession:

O my God, I am ashamed and blush to lift my face to thee,
my God, for our iniquities have risen higher than our heads,
and our guilt has mounted up to the heavens.

— Ezra 9:6

The prophet Jeremiah complained about the way God was treating him. He accused God of being to him "like a deceitful brook, like waters that fail" (Jer. 15:18). The reluctant prophet Jonah expressed his anger to God in a prayer for God to take his life (Jon. 4:1-3). The Psalms are full of expression of the full range of human conditions shared with God in rich detail and extravagant imagery.

In the prayers of the Bible, personal needs and desires are expressed, and there is intercession for other people in need. There are prayers to be saved from one's problems and enemies, and prayers for healing of both mental and physical ills. Sometimes there is a kind of struggle of wills between the human desire and the divine purpose. Self-revelation becomes encounter and confrontation. Prayer in the Bible is sometimes more honest than polite.

The openness with God in scripture is based on the assumption that not only are we affected by God in prayer, but that our prayers also make a difference to God. In the New Testament, the author of James declared, "The prayer of the righteous is powerful and effective" (James 5:16). Since our prayers are directed to God, we must assume that prayer affects God.

One of the striking characteristics of biblical prayer is its honesty. A serious block to prayer is dishonesty, or role-playing with God. All of us play roles. We may fill the role of secretary, dentist, parent, or spouse. And all of us wear masks. They are necessary in our social relationships. But in prayer, roles should be abandoned and masks put aside. God knows our true selves better than we know ourselves. We do not need to play the saint with God, saying all the right things. We do not need to pretend or hide.

Prayer is a matter of honest communication between a genuine "I" and a "Thou" who knows us intimately and loves us unconditionally (even when we role-play!), and who hears us in a way that makes a difference.

FORMS OF PRAYER

Communion with God in prayer takes many forms in the Christian tradition. Words and verbal forms of communication are used in most public worship, although the Society of Friends, or Quakers, are well known for their silent meetings. Prayers in public worship may be strictly prescribed in a standard liturgy, written fresh for each service of worship, created spontaneously in the service, or a combination of these forms depending on the traditions and customs of a worshiping community.

Some people pray in tongues; others chant or use mantras. Prayers can be sung. But prayer without words is possible too. Prayer can take the form of thought or creative visualization or the more passive quiet contemplation. In individual prayer, the beginner may find the use of words necessary. As with a new acquaintance, silence may be awkward. Even words may be awkward. But as the relationship between God and the person in prayer develops and matures, the number of words may decline. As it is possible simply to be together in silence with an intimate friend, so it is possible to be silent in prayer before God.

Prayer is not a special privilege reserved for people who are good with words. How perfectly or imperfectly a person speaks is unimportant in personal prayer. God can hear the profound meanings in our simplest words and read our minds and hearts!

A man regularly spent an hour each day sitting in the front row of a small chapel in his town. One day the minister met him as he left and asked him what he did each day in the chapel. The man pointed to the crucifix hanging over the altar before which he sat, and said, "I just look at him and he looks at me."

As prayer can be both verbal and nonverbal, it can also be both public and private, or corporate and individual. In fact, it is important for the prayer life of the Christian to have both. We are to pray both in our room with the door shut, where our Father who "sees in secret" (Matt. 6:6) will reward us, and in groups gathered together in Christ's name where his presence is in the midst of us (Matt. 18:20).

Kenneth Leech uses the words "solitude" and "solidarity" to describe these two settings for prayer, and he points out that they are "inseparably linked." Each is complementary to the other. As Christians we are called to join with the church in common worship and prayer. We need to share in listening for God's word to the church and to join in the prayers of the community. We need prayers in solidarity with our Christian brothers and sisters. There, as Evelyn Underhill points out, "we are released from a narrow selfish outlook on the universe by a common act of worship."

But public worship can become empty ritual or impersonal form. Prayer in solitude provides the opportunity for interacting with God about the unique business of our own lives. But private prayer needs the guidance and inspiration of common prayer. A person who prays only alone is in danger of drifting into individualistic piety that is something other that Christian faith. Participation in both public and private prayer is essential for wholeness in the experience of Christian prayer.

Whether we pray in the privacy of our room or in community, we are praying as the church. We may pray in solitude but not in isolation. For those who pray in Christ's name are praying as a part of God's people in Christ. In that sense, all prayer—even the prayer of the hermit in the desert or the patient in the nursing home—can be corporate prayer.

There is no such thing as a purely private relationship between a single human being and the "person" of God, for we come as part of Christ's church. We encounter in God our interconnectedness with all that is.

PRAYER IN THE VISION OF GOD

*F*inally, it is important to note the place of prayer in the vision or purpose of God. Jesus' summary of the law in the great commandment begins with the commandment to love God with our whole being (Matt. 22:37). A conscious, intentional relationship with God in prayer is one of the ways this love is expressed and nurtured. Even in our simplest and most elementary prayers, we are doing the will of God.

Prayer is one means of grace. God can work in our lives through the prayer relationship in healing, whole-making, saving ways. Prayer is not a human enterprise. God comes to us. God's spirit works in us, offering this mysterious linking of the divine Spirit with our spirits, making possible this communion of heart with heart. Our part is but to respond to the divine gift. This communion is one of the ways we are called forward to our full humanity and invited to be participants in God's love and grace.

PREPARATION AND CENTERING

O come, let us sing to the Lord;
Let us come into his presence with thanksgiving.
O come, let us worship and bow down, let us kneel
before the Lord, our Maker![23]

PRAISE AND ADORATION

Praise to the Lord, who o'er all things so wondrously
reigning,
bears thee on eagle's wings, e'er in his keeping
maintaining.
God's care enfolds all whose true good he upholds,
Hast thou not known his sustaining?

Praise to the Lord, who dost nourish thy life and
restore thee;
fitting thee well for the tasks that are ever before thee;
Then to thy need God as a mother doth speed,
spreading the wings of grace o'er thee.[24]

I praise you for . . .

CONFESSION

O God, you have set forth the way of life in your beloved
son. I confess with shame my slowness to learn of him, my
reluctance to follow him. You have spoken and called, and I
have not paid attention. Your beauty has shown forth, and I

have been blind. You have stretched out your hands to me through other people, and I have passed by. I have taken great benefits with little thanks. I have been unworthy of your changeless love.... Hear my confession and forgive me of these and all my sins.[25]

MEDITATIVE READING OF SCRIPTURES

Day One:	Matthew 6:9–13
Day Two:	Isaiah 55:6–11
Day Three:	Jeremiah 31:31–34
Day Four:	Jeremiah 15:10–18
Day Five:	Jonah 3:10–4:11
Day Six:	John 15:1–11
Day Seven:	Matthew 18:20

Insights from the scriptures:

PETITIONS

I pray for an awareness of your presence—inspiring, challenging, and giving me strength in these ways . . .

I pray for guidance in the way that leads to true joy, especially in relationship to this part of my life . . .

I pray for help in understanding how to pray for myself in this puzzling situation . . .

I pray for . . .

INTERCESSIONS

I pray for our physical environment. Enhance our reverence for our hospitable but fragile earth. Teach us to live in harmony with the rest of creation and to use its resources wisely. I pray especially for . . .

I pray for those whose lives are closely linked with mine. May they receive the good gifts you have in store for them. I pray for . . .

I pray for those who suffer. Give them healing, comfort, courage and hope. Bring them to the joy of salvation. I pray for . . .

I pray for . . .

THANKSGIVING

O Supreme Lord of the Universe,
    you fill and sustain everything around us.
With the touch of your hand you turned chaos into order,
    darkness into light.
Unknown energies you hid in the heart of matter,
    From you burst forth the splendor of the sun
    and the mild radiance of the moon.
Stars and planets without number you set in ordered
    movement.
You are the source of the fire's heat and the wind's might,
    of the water's coolness and the earth's stability.
Deep and wonderful are the mysteries of your creation.[26]

I thank you for . . .

DEDICATION

> Dear Jesus, in whose life I see
> all that I would, but fail to be;
> let thy clear light forever shine,
> to shame and guide this life of mine.[27]

SILENCE

BENEDICTION

May the God of hope fill you with all joy and peace in believing, so that you may abound in hope by the power of the Holy Spirit. Amen.[28]

CREDITS FOR PRAYER GUIDE FIVE

23. From Psalm 95.

24. From the hymn "Praise to the Lord, the Almighty." Words by Joachim Neander.

25. Adapted from the *Book of Worship for Church and Home.*

26. Adapted from *New Orders of the Mass in India.*

27. John Hunter.

28. Romans 15:13.

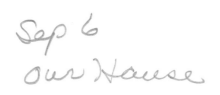

Sep 6
our House

PRAYER AS MEDITATION | 6

PREPARATION AND CENTERING

"*B*e still, and know that I am God," an admonition from the Psalms (46:10), gives us a good starting place for prayer.

"Be still?" responds a chorus of voices. "With all I have to do? That may have been possible for a wandering people camping in the desert at night or for village folk in ancient Palestine. Life was simpler in those days. But in the twentieth-century rat race, that's easier said than done."

Rufus Jones, a twentieth-century American Quaker mystic and social activist, points to the problem of finding time to be still as a major block to the kind of prayer that makes a difference.

> Hush, waiting, meditation, concentration of spirit, are just the reverse of our busy, driving, modern temper. The person who meditates, we are apt to think, will lose an opportunity to do something; while he muses, the procession will go on and leave him behind.

Stillness is not essential to prayer. We can pray in the middle of noise and confusion. But the experience of the church across the centuries has been that "being still" is helpful in enhancing awareness of the presence of God.

Finding or making time to pray is a first and major step. A good place to start is by attending the regular worship services of a congregation of Christian people. Participating in the framework of a worship service—actually engaging in the parts of the service as an active worshiper—can be an easy way to discipline yourself to pray.

A small group in which people share the prayer experience and hold each other accountable for personal spiritual disciplines can provide valuable support and encouragement. The consistent use of a devotional periodical at a set time each day is a pattern used by millions of people. Setting the time and place for prayer is a personal matter and, not surprisingly, for many people this is a major hurdle.

Whatever the time and place of prayer, it is usually a good idea to spend the first few minutes in collecting the mind, relaxing the body, and surrendering the spirit to openness in prayer. The purpose of being still is to know that God is God, to be aware of God's presence with us.

Rufus Jones tells about a group of children on an island just off the New England coast. A visitor decided to have a summer Sunday School for the children. The island was so tiny that the ocean could be seen from every part of it. The children could hear the sound of the surf from the time they woke in the morning until they went to sleep at night. They could smell the salty sea air with every breath. Most of the protein in their diet came from the ocean. They had sailed across its surface in their father's boats, and they had played in its waves on the beaches.

The teacher gathered the children for the first lesson. Beginning with the familiar, the teacher asked, "How many of you have seen the Atlantic Ocean?" The children did not respond. They looked at the teacher blankly, not knowing what he was talking about. The Atlantic Ocean was their constant environment, but nobody had ever named it or interpreted it to them.

This is a parable of our life, says Jones. God is a constant part of our environment. Prayer begins with conscious openness to that presence. It is as if we are sharing a room or a car with someone else. Our attention may be on other things, but we suddenly realize the other is there. "Oh yes, you are here too!" And communication with that other then begins to be the center of our attention. Because God is present with us as spirit rather than as another body, being in touch with our own spirit (centering, being quiet) helps us to be aware, "Oh yes, you are here too!"

Centering is a process of pulling the attention into a focus, so that the mind can move to the heart. Simple awareness exercises may help. You can begin by being aware of your feelings. Identify your own present state of being. How are you at this moment? What is it like to be you right now? Are you happy, angry, depressed, excited, relaxed, anxious? What are you feeling? If you keep a journal, you may want to write down your feelings. If your mind is spinning, take a few minutes to quiet the flow of your thoughts. One technique is to imagine your mind as a whirling system of turning wheels. Visualize the wheels slowing down until they are barely moving. Be aware of your body. Are you tense, feeling pain, tired, tingling? If your body is tense, intentionally relax your muscles. Focus on one part of your body at a time—the face, the neck, the shoulders— deliberately letting go of all of the tenseness there, letting it flow away.

Notice your environment—the sounds you can hear, the odors and fragrances you can smell, other signals of which you are aware. This helps you to center in the present moment, the here and now. Attention to breathing can help you to grow quiet. Taking a few, slow breaths can make deep relaxation possible. Observe the gentle breathing in of cool air through the nostrils and into the lungs and then the breathing out of warm air. Awareness of this natural rhythm in your body, like waves washing an ocean beach, prepares the mind for the inner communion of prayer.

Initially, this centering process may take a few minutes. With practice, centering can be done more quickly and easily. It is good for the body as well as the soul.

In the process of centering, you may become aware of strong feelings, concerns so powerful that it is hard to relax or become quiet. If so, you can begin immediately to share these with God. You may need to spend your prayer time in an honest unburdening of your soul in God's presence, asking for what you need for yourself or desire for others and listening to what God may be saying to you in response. On other days, you may want simply to be quiet in the presence of God.

MEDITATIVE READING OF SCRIPTURE

*P*eople read the Bible for many reasons. Some study it to learn what it has to say. Some read it to analyze it as a piece of literature. Scripture also can be read meditatively, as a way to pray. In meditative reading, or "praying the scriptures," the reader approaches the text listening for the word of God in a personal way. The reader puts himself or herself into the text, looking for the connections between the reader's personal story and God's story.

For example, a meditative reading of the story of the visit of Jesus in the home of Mary and Martha and Lazarus (see Luke 10:38–42), offers opportunity to identify with several characters. You can put yourself in the place of Martha.

As you read the story, reflect on how Martha felt. Then

meditate on how in your life you can identify with Martha. Ask questions like these: Where do I feel anxiety? What is distracting me from giving attention to Jesus? Listen to Jesus' word to Martha, and listen for how God might be speaking to you in this story. Ask: "What is the one thing I need?"

Or you can identify with Mary as you reflect on the story. What is her experience of Jesus, and what are her feelings? How does it feel to welcome Jesus? Imagine yourself sitting at his feet. Look at his face. What do you see? What is that better thing that he is commending in you?

Psalm 139 can be read as a personal prayer, reading it as if it is your own words and reflecting on each verse that seems to speak to you, feeling what it means to be so completely known and understood by God.

In meditative reading of scripture, the message of the passage is encountered not by the head but by the heart. The word is connected directly to one's life.

Sometimes it is helpful to read the passage through once to get the overall picture of the content. Reading a commentary for an understanding of the context and original meaning of the passage can help you put yourself in the place of the original participants. Then a meditative, prayerful-listening type of reading takes you into the passage, giving God's word a chance to feed your spirit.

Reflecting on this experience of praying the scriptures by journaling, or creating artistically, or discussing it in a group may be helpful.

The Benedictine order in the Roman Catholic church has an ancient tradition of prayer that has been instructive to many contemporary Protestants. This is the pattern of *Lectio divina*. This is a structure of four movements for prayerful reading of scripture.

The first movement is *lectio*—receiving the words of scripture like food for life from the table of our Lord. The second movement is *meditatio*—the act of "chewing on the words and tasting the Lord's gift." The third movement is *oratio*— digesting what we can through dialogue with the Lord. The fourth movement is *contemplatio*—abiding in the Presence as we become more deeply one with the Lord in love and service.

Meditative reading of scripture—or praying the scriptures—moves prayer into the listening mode. It serves as a corrective to the tendency to let prayer become nothing more than an outpouring of a personal agenda. Dietrich Bonhoeffer wrote in *Life Together*, "The most promising method of prayer is to allow oneself to be guided by the word of the Scriptures. In this way, we shall not become victims of our own emptiness."

Meditating on scripture, however, is different from looking at a work of art where the artist says that it can mean whatever you want it to mean.

The material in the Bible has come from a variety of sources, spoken and written, using a variety of literary forms for a variety of purposes. The contents of the Bible have been used and shaped over the centuries by a community of faith for worship and instruction. Scholars in recent years have pointed to the value of understanding the setting and the literary form and the function of a particular passage in order to get at its original meaning. Much new light has been thrown on scripture by this scholarly analysis, and some exciting discoveries have been made.

One negative effect of this analytical approach to scripture is that it may prevent people who are not scholars from coming directly to the Bible for their own personal devotional life. The Bible, however, should not be given over to the private custody of the scholars. The Christian in the pew should not be limited to reading scripture through the lenses of Bible scholars.

Many of the passages, themes, and forms that had one meaning when used originally in scripture reappear later with a new meaning and application. The New Testament includes an abundance of quotes and references from the Old Testament. Frequently an entirely new meaning is given to the old words. We do not need to be strictly limited to the original, historical meaning of passages of scripture in our understanding and interpretation of them. The original message is not the only message that it is legitimate for us to hear.

However, Christians do need to be alert to the danger of misusing scriptural materials. Literalism that ignores cultural context, literary form, and canonical themes can produce mis-interpretations that violate the central truths of the Bible. Individual passages can be read to say what we want them to say.

No complete and final set of guidelines for devotional use of the scripture, guaranteed to protect the reader from all error, has yet been developed. While we wait for such help, the Holy Spirit continues to speak to us directly through scripture. We can test our interpretations against the traditions of the Christian community, our reason, and our personal experience. We also have the gifts of interpretation provided by modern scholarship, a great deal of which is easily accessible to lay people.

In meditating about God with scripture, two questions may be helpful. "What does this passage tell me about God? What does this tell me about the possibilities toward which God is calling all of creation, including me?" Such thinking about God and listening for God's word through the Scriptures can lead naturally to prayer or communion with God.

PREPARATION AND CENTERING

Worship God in spirit and truth, for this is what God wants.[29]

PRAISE AND ADORATION

Let all the people praise you, O God!
Your constant love fills the universe,
    and your faithfulness is without limit.
Your righteousness is like the towering mountains;
Your justice is like the depths of the sea.
People and animals and all things are cared for by you.
How precious is your love, O God!
Your people will find protection
    under the shadow of your wings.
We live on the abundance of good things
    that you provide.
With you is the fountain of life,
    and because of your light we see light.
I praise your name, O God.[30]

I praise you, O God, for . . .

CONFESSION

Almighty and most merciful God, I have erred and strayed from your ways like a lost sheep. I have followed too much the devices and desires of my own heart. I have offended against your holy laws. I have left undone those things that I ought to have done, and I have done those things that I ought not to have done. Hear my confession . . .

Have mercy on me. Spare me and restore me according to your promises in Christ Jesus. Grant that I may live a righteous life to the glory of your holy name. Amen.[31]

MEDITATIVE READING OF SCRIPTURE

Day One: Philippians 4:4–7
Day Two: Mark 2:1–12
Day Three: Mark 5:21–34
Day Four: Luke 8:22–25
Day Five: Isaiah 49:13–16
Day Six: Romans 8:38–39
Day Seven: Luke 15:8–10

Insights from the scriptures:

PETITIONS

I pray for daily bread, the necessities of life . . .

I pray for health in body, mind and spirit . . .

I pray for protection from all that might hurt or destroy me . . .

I pray for . . .

INTERCESSIONS

I pray for the church. May all who are part of your church in the world be united in your spirit, speak the truth in love, and show forth your glory in the world . . .

I pray for peace. Teach the people of all nations the ways of justice and peace. Guide them in the ways of mutual respect and give them commitment to serving the common good . . .

I pray for the leaders of our nation and the nations of the world. May they do justice, love mercy, and walk in the way of truth. I pray especially today for . . .

I pray for . . .

THANKSGIVING

O God, you have been gracious to me through all the years of my life. I thank you for your loving care which has filled my days and brought me to this time and place. You have given me life and reason and set me in a world filled with your glory. You have comforted me with family and friends and ministered to me through the hands of my sisters and brothers. You have filled my heart with a hunger after you and have given me your peace. You have redeemed me and called me to a high calling in Christ Jesus. You have given me a place in the fellowship of your Spirit and the witness of your Church. You have been my light in darkness, and a rock of strength in adversity and temptation. You have been the very Spirit of joy in my joys and the all-sufficient reward in all my labors. You have remembered me when I forgot you. You followed me even when I tried to flee from you. You met me with forgiveness when I returned to you. For all your patience and overflowing grace, I praise your holy name, O God.[32]

Today I am especially thankful for . . .

DEDICATION

Lord, make me an instrument of your peace,
Where there is hatred, let me sow love;
Where there is injury, pardon;
Where there is doubt, faith;
Where there is despair, hope;
Where there is darkness, light;
Where there is sadness, joy.

O Divine Master,
Grant that I may not so much
Seek to be consoled as to console;
To be understood as to understand;
To be loved as to love;
For it is in giving that we receive;
It is in pardoning that we are pardoned;
And it is in dying that we are born to eternal life. Amen.[33]

Lord, I commit myself to you in this way today . . .

SILENCE

BENEDICTION

Now may Jesus Christ himself and God our Father, who loved us and through grace gave us eternal comfort and good hope, comfort your heart and strengthen you in every good work and word. Amen.[34]

Credits for Prayer Guide Six

29. John 4:23 (author's paraphrase).

30. Psalm 36:5–9 (author's paraphrase).

31. Adapted from "Prayers of Confession, Assurance, and Pardon" (#891) in *The United Methodist Hymnal.*

32. Adapted from the "Covenant Renewal Service" in *The United Methodist Book of Worship.*

33. Saint Francis of Assisi.

34. 2 Thessalonians 2:16–17 (author's paraphrase).

PRAYER AS PRAISE AND ADORATION AND THANKSGIVING

"Then sings my soul, my Savior God to Thee:
   HOW GREAT THOU ART! HOW GREAT THOU ART!
Then sings my soul, my Savior God, to Thee,
   HOW GREAT THOU ART! HOW GREAT THOU ART!"

The soul sings in praise and adoration, the hymn says. And congregations love to sing about that experience. The soul sings after contemplation of the wonder of God's being.

"O Lord, my God! When I in awesome wonder
consider all the worlds Thy hands have made,
I see the stars, I hear the rolling thunder,
Thy power throughout the universe displayed."

The traditional starting place for community worship of God is this consideration in awesome wonder that expresses itself in praise or adoration. The congregation gathers, opens worship, and launches into the music of praise:

O for a thousand tongues to sing
my great Redeemer's praise,
the glories of my God and King,
the triumphs of his grace.

Holy, holy, holy! Lord God Almighty!
Early in the morning our song shall rise to thee.
Holy, holy, holy! Merciful and mighty,
God in three persons, blessed Trinity!

Joyful, joyful, we adore thee, God of glory, Lord of love.

God of the sparrow,
God of the whale,
God of the swirling stars,
How does the creature say Awe
How does the creature say Praise

Attention is focused on God. God's attributes of glory, holiness, mercy, might, love, and creative power are lifted up and celebrated with the accompanying response of wonder and awe. And joy! No matter what mood, no matter what preoccupations accompanied the worshiper to the service, praise provides a new context, a new setting for one's life.

But praise to God is frequently neglected in personal and private prayer. The tendency is to plunge immediately into the pouring out of needs and desires. Attention is on the concern or problem, and God is off on the sidelines vaguely perceived.

The first petition of our model prayer for good reason is "Hallowed be thy name." Jesus understood our need to begin prayer with this acknowledgement of who it is with whom we have communion. The rest of the prayer conversation flows out of and is shaped by that initial recognition of the nature of the One with whom we communicate.

In praise and adoration, we give our love to God. As in any other relationship, if this is taken for granted, something of indescribable value is lost. The word praise is an appropriate synonym for love in the context of worship.

Expressing our praise and love to God may be awkward at first. We may feel awkward about praise as if we are engaged in just "buttering up" God before getting to the petitions. We may find ourselves at a loss for words. Simple prose hardly seems adequate for the job. What do you say?

Much of the praise and adoration in our tradition is in the form of poetry and song. Our praise to God can be stimulated by reading and reflecting on the praise others have offered to God. Praise hymns and the Psalms are a wonderful source of meditation materials that tune the mind and heart to the joyous experience of praising God. We learn to express our love for God by hearing how others have done it.

Nurture your soul on such passages as these:

> The heavens are telling the glory of God, and the firmament proclaims his handiwork. . . . The law of the Lord is perfect, reviving the soul; the decrees of the Lord are sure, making wise the simple.
>
> — Psalm 19:1, 7

> Sing to the Lord, bless his name; tell of his salvation from day to day. Declare his glory among the nations, his marvelous works among all the peoples. For great is the Lord, and greatly to be praised.
>
> — Psalm 96:2–4

Our praise need not be eloquent. In *Letters to Malcolm: Chiefly on Prayer*, C. S. Lewis recounts a day when the language for praise was no longer a problem.

> You first taught me the great principle (of adoration), "Begin where you are." I had thought one had to start by summoning up what we believe about the goodness and greatness of

God, by thinking about creation and redemption and "all the blessings of this life." You turned to the brook and once more splashed your burning face and hands in the little waterfall and said, "Why not begin with this?"

And it worked. . . . That cushiony moss, that coldness and sound and dancing light were no doubt very minor blessings compared with "the means of grace and the hope of glory." But then they were manifest. So far as they were concerned, sight had replaced faith. They were not the hope of glory, they were the very exposition of glory itself.

Prayers of thanksgiving are easier prayers than prayers of praise and adoration. In fact, giving thanks to God is a good way to begin to learn to pray. Children often learn to pray thanksgiving prayers first and can do this with great imagination. When called upon to pray aloud in a group, even a novice can express thanksgiving to God, and thanksgiving is always appropriate. There is so much for which to be thankful to God even in the most difficult situations.

The Great Thanksgiving in our liturgy for Holy Communion says it well:

> It is right, and a good and joyful thing,
> always and everywhere to give thanks to you,
> Almighty God, creator of heaven and earth.

Thanksgiving is appropriately expressed for all of the gifts of creation. Folliot Pierpoint, more than a century ago, summarized some of these in the hymn "For the Beauty of the Earth."

> For the beauty of the earth,
> For the glory of the skies,

For the love which from our birth
Over and around us lies;

For the beauty of each hour
Of the day and of the night,
Hill and vale, and tree and flower,
Sun and moon, and stars of light;

For the joy of ear and eye,
For the heart and mind's delight,
For the mystic harmony
Linking sense to sound and sight;

For the joy of human love,
Brother, sister, parent, child,
Friends on earth and friends above,
For all gentle thoughts and mild;

For thy church, that evermore
Lifteth holy hands above,
Offering up on every shore
Her pure sacrifice of love;

For thyself, best Gift Divine,
To the world so freely given,
For that great, great love of thine,
Peace on earth and joy in heaven;

Lord of all, to thee we raise,
This our hymn of grateful praise.

Two of the great prayers of our worship tradition are
prayers of thanksgiving—the Great Thanksgiving prayer that is

prayed as the faithful gather at the Lord's table, and the Thanksgiving Over the Water prayer that precedes the sacrament of Baptism. These two prayers recount the record of salvation history, and give thanks for the greatest gift of all—that Gift Divine.

Paul admonished the Christians in Philippi to rejoice always. "Do not worry about anything, but in everything by prayer and supplication WITH THANKSGIVING let your requests be made known to God" (Phil. 4:4,6). Rejoicing comes when no matter what the circumstances, we respond with thanksgiving.

It has been said that a thankful person tastes joy twice—once when it happens, and again when gratitude is expressed to God for the joy.

Thanksgiving for who God is and for God's gifts serves to develop inner strength and hope. As God's goodness is reviewed, the expectation of God's future goodness is enhanced. If God has done all of these good things for us in the past, then surely we can expect that God will continue to do the same in the future.

Both praise and thanksgiving are important in prayer. Praise is addressed to the nature of the Giver. Thanksgiving is addressed to the nature of the gifts. The tragedy is that we make gods of the gifts of life and we forget the Giver. We worship the things God provides and neglect God. We find our identity in hugging God's gifts rather than in the embrace of the Giver. Thanksgiving needs to be balanced with praise.

Beginning prayers of thanksgiving can mature into prayers of praise that express love to God for who God is—without leaving behind the expression of gratitude for all that God does.

Preparation and Centering

For God alone my soul waits in silence.[35]

Someone's praying Lord, come by here.[36]

Praise and Adoration

My soul praises you, O God!
With all my being, I praise your holy name!
I will not forget all your benefits,
You will forgive all of my guilt
    and heal all of my suffering,
You rescue me from the pit of death
    and surround me with love and mercy.
You fill my life with good things,
You judge in favor of the oppressed,
You do not punish us as we deserve,
Your goodness endures to all generations.
My soul praises you, O God![37]

I praise you today for . . .

Confession

Most merciful God, I confess that I have sinned against you in thought, word and deed, by what I have done, and by what I have left undone. I have not loved you with my whole heart; I have not loved my neighbors as myself. I am truly sorry and humbly repent. Hear my confession . . .

For the sake of your Son Jesus Christ, have mercy on me, forgive me, that I may delight in your will, and walk in your ways, to the glory of your name. Amen.[38]

MEDITATIVE READING OF SCRIPTURE

Day One:	Romans 11:33–36
Day Two:	Psalm 100
Day Three:	Psalm 19:1–10
Day Four:	Luke 1:46–55
Day Five:	Psalm 146
Day Six:	Colossians 2:6–7
Day Seven:	Philippians 4:4–7

Insights from the scripture:

PETITIONS

In response to your invitation, I share my troubles, my worries, my deepest needs with you . . .

Open my mind to the ideas, possibilities, relationships, understandings that are your will for me. Lift my vision beyond the boundaries of this world to the horizon of your new possibilities . . .

Help me to purge from my life discrimination against those who are different or in the minority, especially in this situation . . .

I pray for . . .

Intercessions

I pray for your church. May all who have been baptized into its fellowship be filled with your spirit and made perfect in love and good works. I pray especially for . . .

I pray for my family. Teach us to weave those fragile threads of gentle love which eventually combine to create a cable of trust and affection binding us together. I pray today especially for . . .

I pray for those who live with fear because of violence in their communities or in their homes. Help them to find the paths to peace. I pray for . . .

I pray for . . .

Thanksgiving

Eternal Spirit, your never-failing grace is the source of all hope and the lure that tugs me in the direction of all good things. Thank you for the goodness that I do not deserve and cannot earn or repay. Today I am especially thankful for . . .

Dedication

Lord, I want to be a Christian, in my heart. I want to be more loving and like Jesus, in my heart.[39]

Silence

Benediction

May the God of hope fill us with all joy and peace in believing through the power of the Holy Spirit. Amen.

NOTES ON CHAPTER 7

CREDITS FOR PRAYER GUIDE SEVEN

35. Psalm 62:5.
36. From an African-American spiritual.
37. Psalm 103:1–18 (author's paraphrase).
38. Adapted from "Prayers of Confession, Assurance, and Pardon" (#890) in *The United Methodist Hymnal.*
39. From an African-American spiritual.

PRAYER AS CONFESSION 8

A second way we can pray is confession. The prayer of confession is normally combined with a petition for forgiveness. Confession comes low on the popularity list with many Christians and is frequently neglected in personal worship, in spite of the central role confession plays in spiritual growth.

The popular attitude toward confession and repentance is reflected in a Doonesbury comic strip. The Reverend is talking to some prospective members who are inquiring about the basic approach of his Little Church of Walden.

The Reverend says: "I like to describe it as 12-step Christianity. Basically I believe that we're all recovering sinners. My ministry is about overcoming denial, it's about recommitment, about redemption. It's all in the brochure there."

The wife jumps on this. "Wait a minute—sinners? Redemption? Doesn't that imply guilt?"

The Reverend says, "Well, yes, I do rely on the occasional disincentive to keep the flock from going astray. Guilt's a part of that."

The husband joins the discussion. "I dunno, there's so much negativity in the world as it is."

The wife has made up her mind. "That's right, We're looking for a church that's supportive, a place where we can feel good about ourselves. I'm not sure the guilt thing works for us."

The husband holds back. "On the other hand, you do offer racquetball."

But the wife is out the door. "So did the Unitarians, honey. Let's shop around some more."

The prayer of confession has an important place in the tradition of Christian prayer. Jesus includes it in the model prayer in his direction to pray: Forgive us our sins (Luke 11:4).

The Old Testament prophet Isaiah gives an example of confessional prayer in his report of his vision of God in the temple as a young man. Isaiah sees God "high and lofty" (Isa. 6:1). Around God is a chorus singing, "Holy, holy, holy is the Lord of hosts; the whole earth is full of his glory" (Isa. 6:3). Isaiah's response to this vision of a holy God is an overwhelming sense of his own unholiness: "And I said : "Woe is me! I am lost, for I am a man of unclean lips, and I live among a people of unclean lips; yet my eyes have seen the King, the Lord of hosts!" (Isa. 6:5)

The vision continues. One of the beings surrounding God comes to Isaiah with a burning coal "that had been taken from the altar with a pair of tongs" and he "touched my (Isaiah's) mouth with it and said: 'Now that this has touched your lips, your guilt has departed and your sin is blotted out'" (Isa. 6:6-7).

For centuries, people have seen in Isaiah's vision their own experience. In God's presence, their own imperfections have become keenly perceived. Confession to God in the spirit of repentance brings almost instantaneous awareness of God's forgiveness, with a liberating effect, a freeing for new life. Isaiah discovered himself to be now fit for God's service: "Then I heard the voice of the Lord saying, 'Whom shall I send and who will go for us?' And I said, 'Here am I; send me!'" (Isa. 6:8) Echoes of

Isaiah's experience can be heard in this early twentieth-century hymn by John Hunter:

> Dear Jesus, in whose life I see
> All that I would, but fail to be,
> Let thy clear light forever shine,
> To shame and guide this life of mine.
>
> Though what I dream and what I do
> In my weak days are always two,
> Help me, oppressed by things undone,
> O thou, whose deeds and dreams were one!

"All have sinned and fall short of the glory of God," says Paul (Rom. 3:23). And the author of 1 John asserts that "if we say that we have no sin, we deceive ourselves, and the truth is not in us. If we confess our sins, he who is faithful and just will forgive us our sins and cleanse us from all unrighteousness" (1 John 1:8–9).

Mother Teresa of Calcutta, perhaps one of the most Christlike figures of the twentieth century, goes regularly to confession. A television interviewer, aware that Mother Teresa will probably be canonized as a saint by her church after her death, asked why.

"I am a human being and a sinner," she responded, "and so I need to go to confession regularly."

Unfinished business from the past in the form of offenses and omissions for which we must assume some responsibility can burden us down in the present. Repressing feelings of guilt just makes a bad matter worse. Denying our share of the responsibility in an alienated relationship, our contribution to a destructive situation, is denying who we really are. Since God knows what we want to deny, such efforts to escape our own reality cut us off not only from ourselves but also from openness with God. In *Contemplative Prayer*, Thomas Merton speaks of the feeling that one has been abandoned by God which a person can experience when acting in contradiction to his or her true condition.

The prayer of confession is a means to reconciliation. When we are willing to be open to our own truth, with the will to change our ways and to make amends, God's forgiveness can set us free. Remember the story of the prodigal son, and listen to the words of Psalm 103.

> The Lord is merciful and gracious,
>> slow to anger and abounding in steadfast love.
> He will not always accuse,
>> nor will he keep his anger forever.
> He does not deal with us according to our sins,
>> nor repay us according to our iniquities.
> For as the heavens are high above the earth
>> so great is his steadfast love toward those who fear him;
>> as far as the east is from the west,
>> so far he removes our transgressions from us.
>> — Psalm 103:8–12

Henry Ward Beecher, a notable American preacher of the nineteenth century, talked about the "Nobility of Confession." He said that, although we often think of confession as humbling, even degrading, that there is nothing more noble than recognizing a wrong, feeling and expressing sorrow for it, and renouncing it.

Confession is painful only as long as you fight it. The more difficult part of confession is not doing it. The rewards come when you do. Beecher says that when you have been honest with God, yourself, and each other by confessing your sins, you "breathe the very breath of heaven."

How shall we make our confession? Alcoholics Anonymous has discovered the central importance of confession in the process of recovering from addiction to alcohol. In their "Twelve Steps" program, seven of the steps have to do with getting in touch with one's own reality through confession. Their experience reflects the broad Christian tradition.

THE TWELVE STEPS

Step One: We admitted we were powerless over alcohol—that our lives had become unmanageable.

Step Two: Came to believe that a Power greater than ourselves could restore us to sanity.

Step Three: Made a decision to turn our will and our lives over to the care of God *as we understood Him.*

Step Four: Made a searching and fearless moral inventory of ourselves.

Step Five: Admitted to God, to ourselves, and to another human being the exact nature of our wrongs.

Step Six: Were entirely ready to have God remove all these defects of character.

Step Seven: Humbly asked him to remove our shortcomings.

Step Eight: Made a list of all persons we had harmed, and became willing to make amends to them all.

Step Nine: Made direct amends to such people wherever possible, except when to do so would injure them or others.

Step Ten: Continued to take personal inventory and when we were wrong, promptly admitted it.

Step Eleven: Sought through prayer and meditation to improve our conscious contact with God, as we understood Him, praying only for knowledge of His will for us and the power to carry that out.

Step Twelve: Having had a spiritual awakening as the result of these steps, we tried to carry this message to alcoholics, and to practice these principles in all our affairs.

Self-searching ideally becomes a regular habit in the supportive community of an Alcoholics Anonymous group.

Confession to God needs to include our participation in corporate sins. In Isaiah's vision in the temple, he confesses both, "I am a man of unclean lips," and "I live among a people of unclean lips." He felt both his personal sin and his participation in social sin. Personal confession appropriately includes one's participation in social evils such as institutional racism and pollution of the environment. As the song "Carefully Taught" from the musical *South Pacific* points out, we learn from the time we are very young "to hate all the people [our] relatives hate." As we carry these hatreds unexamined into maturity, we share in the social sin of prejudice. As we practice the wasteful and self-indulgent lifestyle of an affluent society, we share in the deprivation and damage it causes.

Confession does not need to be a matter of wallowing in guilt or of self-flagellation. Confession can be thought of as a way of getting in touch with the growing edges of your Christian pilgrimage. Confession does not need to be preoccupation with the failures of the past. It can be an experience of acknowledging that you are off the track, and asking God to get you back on track.

In the account of John the Baptist in Matthew's gospel

(Matt. 3:2), John the prophet preaches, "Repent, for the kingdom of heaven has come near." Something better is available. Turn from what has been to what can be. Repentance is a future-oriented experience, involving liberation from a sinful past in order to be able to take advantage of the kingdom that has come near.

John sets before his listeners the good, with the clear understanding that they must make a radical turnabout in mind and heart in order to be ready for what is to be. Getting ready for the kingdom means regret for sin and genuine commitment to break with the evil with which you have been engaged. Confession clears the way.

Confession is a matter of acknowledging our reality to God who already knows and accepts us. Once we have confessed and repented, we can leave what has been to God, who offers forgiveness and new possibilities for our lives.

The more difficult part may be forgiving ourselves. When guilt continues to burden the spirit, some other problem may be involved. Guilt that is not relieved by confession and repentance may be neurotic guilt. Counseling or therapy may be necessary to get at its roots and to facilitate its release. Confessing to another person who can be trusted may help to sort out the problem. The Alcoholics Anonymous system of sponsors and the Roman Catholic sacrament of confession testify to the value of working through guilt in dialogue with another person.

God's healing, whole-making, saving power can be at work in us in our prayers of confession and repentance. Like the prophet Isaiah, we can be set free to redirect our energies in more constructive directions. The author of James tells us: "Therefore confess your sins to one another, and pray for one another, so that you may be healed" (James 5:16).

As we praise God and confess to God in prayer, we are turning toward reality—the reality that heals. In praise we open ourselves to God's reality, in confession to our own reality.

In the familiar words of Henry Van Dyke:

> Joyful, joyful, we adore thee,
> God of glory, Lord of love;
> Hearts unfold like flowers before thee,
> Opening to the sun above.
> Melt the clouds of sin and sadness;
> Drive the dark of doubt away;
> Giver of immortal gladness,
> Fill us with the light of day.

PREPARATION AND CENTERING

You have been raised to life with Christ; so set your heart on the things that have been revealed in him.[40]

PRAISE AND ADORATION

Eternal God, I adore you, whose name is love,
    whose nature is compassion, whose presence is joy,
    whose Word is truth, whose Spirit is goodness,
    whose holiness is beauty, whose will is peace,
    whose service is perfect freedom,
    and in knowledge of whom stands our eternal life.
To you be all honor and all glory,
    through Jesus Christ our Lord.[41]

I praise you for . . .

CONFESSION

Heavenly parent, who by your love has made me, and through your love has kept me, and in your love would make me perfect; I humbly confess that I have not loved you with all my heart and soul and mind and strength, and that I have not loved others as Christ has loved me. Your life is within my soul, but my selfishness has hindered you. I have not lived by faith. I have resisted your Spirit. I have neglected your inspirations. Hear my confession . . .

Forgive what I have been; amend what I am, and in your Spirit direct what I shall be; that you may come to the full glory of your creation in me and in all people; through Jesus Christ our Lord. Amen.[42]

MEDITATIVE READING OF SCRIPTURE

Day One: Psalm 51:1–12
Day Two: 2 Corinthians 5:17–21
Day Three: Romans 7:14–8:4
Day Four: Isaiah 6:1–8
Day Five: 1 Timothy 1:12–17
Day Six: Luke 15:1–10
Day Seven: Psalm 32

Insights from the scripture . . .

PETITIONS

Save me from the worship of idols—money, success, power, relevance, popularity, another person . . .

Save me from clouding the sky of my own life and the lives of others with criticism and complaining . . .

With the psalmist, I pray for the joy that comes from your salvation . . .

I pray for . . .

Intercessions

I pray for those who have experienced loss. Surround them with your love, comfort them with your presence and give them your peace. I make this prayer especially for . . .

I pray for our nation. Bless us with your wisdom, so that the poor may not be oppressed and the rich may not be oppressors. Make this a nation having no ruler except God, a nation having no authority but that of Love.[43]

I pray for your church. Touch us with the wonder of Christ's love, and send us out to do what he would do . . .

I pray for . . .

Thanksgiving

Now thank we all our God,
    with heart and hands and voices,
who wondrous things has done,
    in whom this world rejoices;
who from our mothers' arms
    has blessed us on our way
with countless gifts of love,
    and still is ours today.[44]

I thank you for . . .

Dedication

God be in my head, and in my understanding;
God be in my eyes, and in my looking;
God be in my mouth, and in my speaking;

God be in my heart, and in my thinking;
God be at my end, and at my departing.[45]

Silence

Benediction

God's peace, which is far beyond our human understanding, will keep your heart and mind safe in union with Christ Jesus. Amen.[46]

NOTES ON CHAPTER 8

CREDITS FOR PRAYER GUIDE EIGHT

40. Colossians 3:1 (author's paraphrase).

41. Adapted from *The Book of Worship*.

42. Adapted from "Prayers of Confession, Assurance, and Pardon" (#892) in *The United Methodist Hymnal*.

43. Toyohiko Kagawa.

44. From the hymn "Now Thank We All Our God." Words by Martin Rinkhart.

45. Sarum Primer.

46. Philippians 4:7 (author's paraphrase).

PRAYER AS PETITION AND INTERCESSION 9

*T*he most popular way to pray is to ask God for what we want for ourselves and for others. These are prayers of petition and prayers of intercession. Here the yearnings of the heart are expressed in openness with God. Prayers of petition and intercession are expressions of trust in a loving God.

Not only are these the most popular dimensions of prayer, but they are the subjects of most of the questions about prayer: If we ask, what can we expect in terms of answers? Are there limits to what it is appropriate to ask for ourselves and others? How do we understand unanswered prayers?

JESUS TEACHES AND MODELS PRAYER OF PETITION AND INTERCESSION

*J*esus taught his disciples to ask God for things in prayer. In the Lord's Prayer, he directed them to ask for a variety of things: daily bread, forgiveness, and protection. And he modeled petition and intercession in his own prayers. In the prayers reported in the Gospels, he prayed more for others than for himself. But he did ask God for what he needed. And he was clear in his expressions to God about what he wanted for others.

Jesus subordinated his own prayers to the will of God. In doing this, he made an important distinction between Christian prayer and primitive magic. For many people, to pray is to ask. This is a complete and adequate definition of prayer. In extreme cases, prayer can become nothing more than a way of employing super-human powers to get what you want when obtaining it seems to be beyond your human reach.

In a television interview, a coach was asked what he planned to do to prepare for a game in which the odds were against him three to one. He answered, "Pray a lot."

A cartoon featured two fish in a fishbowl over which a menacing cat was crouching. Eyeing a nearby telephone, one fish suggested, "Let's try Dial-a-Prayer!"

On the golf course, a minister made a "hole in one." His golfing partner stammered, "Don't tell me you haven't been praying!"

Christian petition differs from magic in one major way. In Christian prayer, the goal is to communicate with God rather than to manipulate God. The individual's will is asserted and expressed in order that it can be harmonized with God's vision and purpose. In Christian prayer, we tell God what we think we and others want and need. But these petitions are set in the context of a commitment to God. Jesus prayed, "Your will be done" before he prayed "Give us this day our daily bread" (Matt. 6:10–11). In Gethsemane, he qualified his agonizing plea to "let this cup pass from me" (Matt. 26:39) with "your will be done" (Matt. 26:42).

But Jesus also encouraged assertiveness in praying for yourself and for others. In the parable about the woman who besieged an unjust judge, Luke says that Jesus taught his disciples "to pray always and not to lose heart" (Luke 18:1). A Syrophoenician woman, by her assertiveness, convinced Jesus to change his mind and grant her request to free her daughter from a demon (see Mark 7:25–30). Jesus affirmed the boldness of the woman with an issue of blood who reached out from the crowd to touch his robe in the belief she would be healed. Jesus said, "Daughter, your faith has made you well; go in peace" (see Luke 8:43–48).

OPENNESS WITH GOD

*A*ssertiveness in praying for yourself and others is a form of being open with God. The prayer of petition or intercession is self-expression in terms of telling God clearly and completely what you want or need in a particular situation. It is a way of saying, "Here is the way I see this situation, and what my best judgment is about what needs to happen here."

If we do not assert our will in prayer, it may be that God will not be able to offer us possibilities that would be available to us if we expressed our will with strength.

P. T. Forsyth, a famous British preacher of another generation, warned against letting our prayer be simply a total passivity before the will of God. Accepting a situation too quickly as God's will may be more a sign of weakness or immaturity than of faith and trust. Prayer is a matter of encounter of wills—the human will and God's will. Assertiveness is quite appropriate in our prayers.

Forsyth also warned against being too timid in our prayers, too cautious in what we consider permissible subjects for petition. In his book *The Soul of Prayer*, Forsyth says, "Take everything to (God) that exercises you." Speaking of the intimate nature of our communion with God, he continues, "Faith means confidence between you (and God), and not only favours. And there is not confidence if you keep back what is hot or heavy on your heart."

Our Hebrew ancestors often had negative feelings, doubts, fears, grief, frustration, resentment, even anger toward God. There is no reason why this cannot be true for us. Being open with God in prayer will include dealing honestly with the issues of our lives, the things we are working on at the growing edges of our existence. All of that may not be pleasant to hear. But what close relationship is all sweetness and light?

Georgia Harkness, a twentieth-century American theologian, joins P. T. Forsyth in encouraging boldness in prayer. In *Prayer and the Common Life*, she declares that it is fitting for any important need to be expressed to God in prayer. There is no need to limit the categories for our petitions. Needs in all dimensions of our lives are objects of God's concern. We can pray for what we need physically, mentally, socially, and spiritually.

Harkness does add one pertinent word of warning to her encouragement to be bold in prayer. Prayer is misused when we think of it as a way to evade responsibility. We should not pray for food, clothing, shelter, or other material things without making the effort to provide these needs for ourselves. In general, however, timidity and caution are the enemies of prayer.

We can expect that our petitions will be changed in the process of prayer about them. Our wishes and desires may be clarified, purified, and matured. In the process of making our needs known to God, it may be helpful to ask, "Is there a deeper need behind my request? What is it that I really want?" The prayer itself may change several times in the process of being prayed before it can be answered in the context of God's broader vision. The starting place is "confidences," expecting purification in the process of praying, rather than trying to do the screening before beginning to pray.

Creative visualization is an increasingly popular way to pray for one's own needs and the needs of others. Instead of simply rehashing the problem or lamenting the situation, visualizing the ideal solution or the desired outcome can clarify the real need. Such positive imaging can sometimes help the one who prays to see ways to become the answer to one's own prayers. Positive visualization in prayer is more than autosuggestion. It is a way of clearly communicating with God what we need and want.

PETITION

*I*s praying for yourself a selfish thing to do? Jesus did not seem to think so. God's gift of prayer is a gift of relationship. In a relationship we share openly who we are, and our wants and needs are clearly central to who we are. In praying for ourselves, we take seriously the gift of our own lives as well as the responsibility of being good stewards of this gift. We ask God's help in making of our lives the best possible expressions of God's will. In praying for ourselves, we take seriously God's love for us, and we open a way for that love to enter our lives.

An African-American spiritual says it well: "It's me, it's me, it's me, O Lord, standing in the need of prayer." My brother and my sister and the preacher and the deacon and my father and my mother may all be standing in the need of prayer too. But as one of God's children on the pilgrimage through life, I'm standing in the need of prayer every day!

The simplest details of daily life as well as the momentous decisions and major crises that come our way are appropriate subjects for intentional conversation with God. The Christian life can be thought of as an ongoing dialogue between the Christian and God in which everything is included.

INTERCESSION

*P*raying for others is one of the ways we can love our neighbors as ourselves. We can express love by giving to other people, by respecting their human dignity, by protesting and resisting those things that are destructive to human welfare, by ministering to human needs and working for better social conditions, by simple thoughtfulness and consideration. We can also love our neighbors by praying for them.

Prayer for each other is made possible by faith that we are all interconnected with each other in our mutual relationship with a God whose nature is love. It seems that physicists, philosophers, and mystics are all talking about the organismic unity of reality. Contemporary physics has revealed to us a physical reality of interconnectedness in the universe. No person or thing is an island of independence.

The distant moon affects the tides. A tiny virus in one remote country triggers an international epidemic. Every particle of energy is a part of a field of force that is in turn related to larger and larger fields of force through the universe. Everything we do affects the rest of reality. Evelyn Underhill (in *The Collected Writings of Evelyn Underhill*, edited by Lucy Menzies) relates this to prayer:

> The whole possibility of intercessory prayer seems based on this truth of spiritual communion—the fact that we are not separate little units but deeply interconnected—so that all we do, feel and endure has a secret effect, radiating far beyond ourselves.

God's love, which makes prayer for ourselves possible, is equally given to the people we love. God's love is given to the people who are like us and to the people who are different from us. It is given to those who are unattractive to us and to those who threaten us—to our enemies. God's care extends to the sparrows and the lilies of the field, to the trees and the stones, to the atoms and the quarks and the photons. Our neighbor can be understood to be the whole of creation. We are interconnected in God's love with all that is.

When we pray for others, we join our psychic energy, our hearts, to the love of God in active benevolence. How this "works" remains a mystery. Archbishop William Temple has been quoted as saying, "When I pray, coincidences happen; when I don't, they don't!"

At the least, in our prayers of intercession for others, we open ourselves to God's love for them. In so doing, we create the possibility of change in our attitudes toward them, and we make ourselves available as the instruments of God's love in their lives. In addition, we contribute our resources to the supply of love and caring in the world.

Praying for someone else can give direction to our efforts on their behalf. As we share our concern for them, we may receive new insight into what we can do. Our sensitivity may be enhanced and our motivation strengthened. Sometimes intercessory praying is all that we can do. We can pray with faith that, in cooperation with God's creative and healing love, forces are being released in ways that are beyond our understanding.

Our intercessory prayers should reach beyond those for whom we feel natural love. "Love your enemies," said Jesus, "do good to those who hate you, bless those who curse you, pray for those who abuse you" (Luke 6:27–28). He demonstrated this love as he prayed from the cross, "Father, forgive them, for they do not know what they are doing" (Luke 23:34).

By praying for persons to whom we are not attracted or by whom we are threatened, we are drawn beyond our limited self-concern. We can see them against the background of their relationship with God. We can join with God in willing for them good things. Such intercession in the spirit of Christ has the power of creative transformation.

God receives and uses the good wishes for others that we offer in prayer, both in responding to us and in responding to those for whom we pray. God hears us when we bring the needs of others in our prayers. Alfred North Whitehead shares this insight in *Process and Reality*: "What is done in the world is transformed into a reality in heaven, and the reality in heaven passes back into the world. By reason of this reciprocal relation, the love in the world passes into the love in heaven, and floods back again into the world."

Most of what has been said so far has assumed the simplest type of intercession—one person praying for another. But intercession for people in groups, organizations, institutions, and problem situations are all appropriate objects for our intercession. The liturgical prayers of the church have traditionally included prayers for the sick, the poor, the troubled, the lonely, victims of war, and other people in special circumstances of need.

Such intercession involves positive thinking. Intercessory prayers that consist of thinking about all of the problems and pains and negative dimensions of a situation contribute nothing positive to either God or the world. Careful attention to what the other is experiencing and empathy with the other's pain is an important part of preparation for intercession. Intercession itself involves sharing in the loving will of God. Visualization of our best wishes is one way to do this. Another way is to express hopes and wishes in words.

As we pray for the poor, we may find that God is leading us to envision and hope for an economic order in which all human beings will have access to the necessities of life. As we pray for victims of war, we may find ourselves led to envision peace and human community where justice is guaranteed for all. Prayers of intercession lead us to the petition, "Your kingdom come, your will be done" (Matt. 6:10). And this prayer, of course, may be answered as we discover that we can make a contribution to alleviating some of the suffering about which we have shared our concern with God.

We should be willing to be led by the Spirit into interceding not only for those for whom we have a natural concern, but to share in God's concern for all the suffering of the world. Then our prayers will more nearly reflect the spirit of the Lord's prayer.

UNANSWERED PRAYER

*W*hen we pray for ourselves and others, we can trust the answers to God. God hears and takes account of our prayers. The answer may not be exactly what we asked, or what we asked for at all. The answer may resemble "No" as far as we can understand the situation. But God can be trusted to answer. And the answer can be expected to be consistent with God's overall creative and redemptive purposes in the circumstances about which we pray, much of which is known only to God.

Consider again the accounts of Jesus at prayer. In the Garden of Gethsemane, he prayed with great passion to be spared the agony of the cross. Jesus could see his own limited part of the whole picture. He could see the suffering he would have to endure. God could see the larger picture. God knew that he had sent his son into the world that through him the world might be saved. The cross was an essential component of the larger plan. As far as Jesus could see, the answer to the Gethsemane prayer was "No." But in God's view, the answer was an eternal "Yes" to all humankind. The final prayer of Jesus is from the cross: "Father, into your hands I commend my spirit." Here is the prayer of trust in God's good will even in the face of a puzzling example of unanswered prayer.

Christian prayers of petition and intercession, no matter how clearly assertive and passionate, are not demands placed upon God. They are the expressions of the best perceptions of the heart from the creature to the Creator. The answers are often beyond our comprehension, but they can be trusted to be expressions of God's good will for the whole creation.

PREPARATION AND CENTERING

Worship God in the beauty of holiness; serve God with gladness, all the earth.[47]

PRAISE AND ADORATION

I will praise you, O God, with all my heart;
I will tell of all the wonderful things you have done;
I will sing with joy because of you,
You are fair and honest in your judgments,
You rule the world with righteousness,
You judge the nations with justice,
You are a refuge for the oppressed, a place of safety
    in times of trouble,
Those who know you will trust you,
You do not abandon anyone who comes to you.
I will praise you, O God, with all my heart.[48]

I praise you for . . .

CONFESSION

Be merciful to me, O God,
because of your constant love.
I have sinned against you—only against you—
    and done what you consider evil.
So you are right in judging me.
Hear my confession . . .

Remove my sin, and I will be clean.
Create a pure heart in me, O God,
    and put a new and loyal spirit in me.[49]

MEDITATIVE READING OF SCRIPTURE

Day One:	Psalm 42
Day Two:	Luke 8:40–48
Day Three:	I Samuel 1:1–2:11
Day Four:	Matthew 7: 7–11
Day Five:	Luke 18:1–8
Day Six:	Ephesians 3:14–19
Day Seven:	Colossians 1:9–14

Insights from the scripture:

PETITIONS

Plant your word in my heart. Nourish it and make it grow and bear fruit in my life. Prune from me all that is not fruitful.

I pray especially for . . .

I pray for vision to see the way I should go through this perplexing circumstance . . .

I pray for . . .

Intercessions

I pray for those who are experiencing pain in relationships. Take away the hostility and bitterness, and break down the walls that divide and separate. Build up the bonds of love that unite us, and use all of our relationships to serve your purposes on earth. I remember especially . . .

I pray for those whose needs are described in the news today. . .

I pray for those whose needs are known only to themselves, the lonely, the proud, and the isolated. Help me to reach out hands of compassion. Give me strength to help the burdens of my sisters and brothers, especially the burden carried by . . .

I pray for those who are close to me and whose needs I observe on a regular basis. I remember especially . . .

I pray for . . .

I commit these prayers to you, trusting that your answers will be better than my asking.

Thanksgiving

O God, I see you before me at all times. You are near and I will not be troubled. So I am filled with gladness, and my words are full of joy. And I, mortal though I am, will rest assured in hope. You have shown me the paths that lead to life, and your presence fills me with joy. For these and all of your good gifts, I am thankful.[50]

DEDICATION

> O Christ, my only Savior,
> so come to dwell in me that I may go forth
> with the light of your hope in my eyes,
> and with your faith and love in my heart.[51]

SILENCE

BENEDICTION

The Lord bless you and keep you. The Lord make his face to shine upon you and be gracious to you. The Lord lift up his countenance upon you and give you peace. Amen.[52]

Notes on Chapter 9

without love you have nothing

CREDITS FOR PRAYER GUIDE NINE

47. Psalm 96:9 (author's paraphrase).

48. Adapted from Psalm 9 (TEV).

49. Psalm 51:1, 4, 7, 10 (TEV).

50. Adapted from Acts 2:25–26, 28 (TEV).

51. Adapted from a prayer "For the Mind of Christ" in *The United Methodist Book of Worship*.

52. Numbers 6:24–26.

THE DIFFERENCE PRAYER MAKES | 10 |

*T*he television camera focused on Mother Teresa of Calcutta. Seated in a private jet, she was writing a letter. The narrator described how she handles the business of her worldwide religious order of one hundred thousand members with handwritten correspondence delivered by regular mail. She was hitching a ride to look at some of her work in another Indian city. A bemused male voice from another part of the plane asked, "Where do you get all of your energy, Mother?"

She lifted her head. Her tranquil face was framed by her blue and white habit. "That's why we go to the mass," she said. "We start the day with Him and we end the day with Him." Members of her order work with the lepers, the indigent dying, the orphans, the poor of India. Those who live in the mother house in Calcutta are expected to be back from their day's work in time to be present at the evening worship. "We're not social workers, you know," she explains. Christian worship makes the difference.

PRAYER MAKES A DIFFERENCE TO THE ONE WHO PRAYS

*P*rayer is one means of grace—one of the ways in which God's healing, saving, whole-making work is done in the world. Prayer is given to us as a gift from God.

When we appropriate the gift for ourselves, it can make a difference in our lives.

Martin Heidegger, the existentialist philosopher, has described two modes of being-in-the-world. The first is one he termed as unauthentic because personal projects are set for one by others—by social expectations or past conditioning or the hope of reward. The second is the authentic mode in which a person chooses his or her own projects. The Christian, however, has a third option—a mode of being in which one chooses to create one's own life in dialogue with God.

Social pressures push and pull us in all directions. We are motivated to keep up with the Joneses, to be accepted by the in-group, to be loved by desirable people. What we do can be powerfully influenced by what the Joneses, the in-group, or desirable people do, or by what we are told they expect. Much of commercial advertising hooks into our sensitivity to social expectations.

Past conditioning can set unrealistic limits on us, establish us in destructive behavior patterns, and cause us to make faulty assumptions. The reward system of our society can entice us into doing things that violate both ourselves and our environment.

Other-directedness is to some degree desirable and unavoidable. Living cooperatively with other people involves negotiating our projects with the needs and expectations of others. Social expectations, conditioning, and reward systems make possible social existence. But life lived simply in unexamined response to the pressures exerted on us is not our only possibility. We do have the freedom to direct our lives from within. We can choose how to respond to all of the influences in our lives. We can establish our own value system and act out of it. We can choose how much power to give to the various forces at work on us.

One influence on our lives is the presence and call of God. God is with us, exerting an influence on us whether we choose to pay attention or not. When we choose to respond to God's offer of open communication, we choose to give power or weight to that relationship. We make an intentional move to give attention to the ideal possibilities that God offers to us. Without relinquishing our free will, we can freely choose to be Christian disciples. We can choose to live authentically in dialogue with God. Such open communion with God can creatively transform our lives.

In his letter to the church at Corinth, Paul talked about three qualities of the Christian life, or fruits of the spirit: faith, hope, and love (1 Cor. 13:13). When we pray, we open the way for the Spirit to nurture in us all three of these qualities.

PRAYER NURTURES FAITH

*I*n a human friendship, communication and interaction are necessary if the relationship is to survive and grow. I need to know you in order to trust you. The only way we can get acquainted is by trusting each other enough to reveal ourselves. A little trust makes possible the first steps of friendship. This initial acquaintance makes possible more trust, which makes possible deeper friendship. So it is with prayer and faith. Faith expressed in prayer opens the way for the Spirit to nurture new faith, which in turn makes possible new adventures in prayer.

Thomas Merton pointed to this interdependence between prayer and faith in his remarks to a group of monks at a

California monastery. According to Michael Terry, a member of that group of monks, Merton advised:

> Start where you are and deepen what you already have and you realize that you are already there. Everything has already been given to us in Christ. The trouble is that we don't know what we have. All we need is to experience what we already possess. The problem is that we don't slow down and take time to know it.

PRAYER NURTURES HOPE

The Spirit also has an opportunity to nurture hope in us when we pray. Charles Wesley sang of his faith:

> Jesus, my strength, my hope,
> On thee I cast my care,
> With humble confidence look up,
> And know thou hearest my prayer.
> Give me on thee to wait,
> Till I can all things do,
> On thee, almighty to create,
> Almighty to renew.

In a discussion of worship in *Wrestle of Religion with Truth*, Henry Nelson Wieman remembered a street car that operated in Los Angeles in the early part of this century. At one point along its route it climbed a hill.

> The hill is so steep that the car cannot use a trolley. It is lifted by a steel cable which runs endlessly beneath the car and between the rails. But the car does not move until it connects

with the cable in the proper manner. The car stands still until its passengers are in, then a certain clamping mechanism closes down upon the cable and the car is lifted to the top of the hill.

Worship, he says, is the way we clamp down on the cable. When we pray, we discover that we are not alone. We are in God, and God is in us. We do not have to climb our hills in our own strength alone. We can tap into God's resources for our life. The resources of prayer are a source of hope.

In his sermon at Pentecost, Peter quoted from the Psalms, referring to the hope given by an awareness of God's presence.

> I saw the Lord always before me, for he is at my right hand so that I will not be shaken; therefore my heart was glad and my tongue rejoiced; moreover my flesh will live in hope. . . . You have made known to me the ways of life; you will make me full of gladness with your presence.
> — Acts 2:25–26, 28

A person who approaches life hopefully is more likely to be open to the new possibilities offered by God than is a person who is burdened with discouragement, locked in the grip of fear, and inhibited by doubts. Communion with the "almighty to create, almighty to renew" is a channel for the sustenance of hope, a source of strength and energy, a medium through which the Spirit can be preparing us to receive possibilities that we might not otherwise perceive.

In *The Meaning of Prayer*, Harry Emerson Fosdick illustrated the hope-inducing power of prayer with the story of Jem Nicholls, who was influenced by the work of a Mr. Quintin Hogg among the boys of London.

When Jem was asked, after Mr. Hogg's death, how the fight for character was coming on, he said, "I have a bit of trouble in keeping straight, but I thank God all is well. You see, I carry a photo of 'Q. H.' with me always, and whenever I am tempted, I take it out and his look is a wonderful help, and by the grace of God I am able to overcome all."

In prayer we discover that we have more than the resources with which our past has equipped us for facing the hills we have to climb.

PRAYER NURTURES LOVE

*W*hen we pray, we give the Holy Spirit a chance to nurture love in us. Three kinds of love are involved: (1) a healthy kind of self-esteem or respect and appreciation for the unique persons we have been created to be, (2) a corresponding esteem for our human brothers and sisters combined with a willingness to care for them, and (3) a deepening love for and commitment to God.

LOVE FOR OURSELVES

*C*hurch members occasionally object to the inclusion of a prayer of confession in the order of worship for the congregation. "It makes people feel bad," they say. "Confessing our offenses and our negligence stirs up guilt feelings and contributes to low self-esteem. People come to church to feel better, not to feel worse."

Christian confession, however, is a means of grace. When we confess who we are to the One who already knows us and loves us as we really are, we have a chance at self-esteem grounded in personal integrity. God's acceptance and forgiveness does not say that everything we have done and left undone is all right. It says that we can pick up from here and move on. Freed from the burden of guilt, we can live with our real, sinful selves, accepting ourselves because God accepts us and esteeming ourselves because if God prizes us, how can we do otherwise?

Our prayers of confession open the way for God's forgiveness to be operative in our lives. Confession makes an important contribution to the development of healthy self-love.

LOVE FOR OTHERS

*P*rayers of intercession make a contribution to the development of our love for others. Our ability to love other people grows with practice. We learn to love by giving love. In our prayers of intercession, we express our care and concern for other people to God, who also loves and is concerned for them. If I pray for you, the Holy Spirit has an opportunity to be at work in me, increasing my love and concern for you. My prayer may be answered with a fresh insight about what I can do to contribute to your well-being. As I express my love for you, my love can grow.

Prayers for people for whom we have little concern may give the Holy Spirit an opportunity to nurture love and concern for them in us. Prayers for our enemies give the Holy Spirit a chance to show us ways to deal constructively with the conflict or enmity between us. Acting on such insights opens the way for improved relationship and moves us in the direction of love.

At the least, prayers of intercession stretch us beyond self-centeredness and widen the horizons of our concern. As we open ourselves to God's love for other people, some of that compassion may rub off on us. Mother Teresa, for example, says that she sees Christ dying in the gutters of Calcutta. When we give God a chance, we may find ourselves sent out as agents of divine love.

LOVE FOR GOD

When we pray, we give the Holy Spirit an opportunity to increase love for God in us. When we take time for adoration, praise, and thanksgiving, we open ourselves to more profound comprehension of who God is and what God does. An expanded and clarified vision of God has enhanced power to evoke devotion from us. As we grow in prayer, our increased experience with God can lead to a deeper love for God. This, at least, is the witness of the saints of the church.

Other words besides faith and hope and love have been used to describe the work of the Holy Spirit in the one who communicates openly with God. Trust, confidence, power, strength, patience, peace, tranquility of soul, personal integration, an attitude of gratitude, even "recharged batteries" are identified as by-products of prayer. And there is abundant testimony that through the life of prayer, the spirit of Christ can come into a human life. William James once said that we become like what we attend to.

When we open ourselves in prayer, we respond to the invitation offered in Revelation 3:20: "Listen, I am standing at the door knocking; if you hear my voice and open the door, I will come in to you and eat with you, and you with me."

Paul speaks about the Spirit dwelling in us: "If the Spirit of him who raised Jesus from the dead dwells in you, he who raised Christ from the dead will give life to your mortal bodies also through his Spirit that dwells in you" (Rom. 8:11). Sometimes it is Christ who dwells in us. "To them God chose to make known how great among the Gentiles are the riches of the glory of this mystery, which in Christ in you, the hope of glory" (Col. 1:27). And sometimes Paul speaks of growing up into Christ, or putting on Christ (Gal. 3:27). The gospel writer John, on the other hand, reports that Christ spoke of himself as the vine, his human disciples as the branches (John 15:5).

In multiple ways the message is communicated that God can live in and through us. As we practice being open to God, the divine likeness can grow in us. Our desires can be purified, a new value system can evolve, we can become new people. In *The Jesus Prayer*, Per-Olof Sjogren reports that:

> When (Christ) lives in my heart, then he also shines through; when praise of him is singing in my heart, then it also rings through, often without my knowing. It is not my personality but his that becomes luminous.

All that can be said to this point about the difference prayer makes to an individual can be said also about the church. As the church opens to God in prayer, it gives the Holy Spirit an opportunity to nurture its faith, its hope, its love, and to make it the body of Christ in the world.

But the experience of praying together has the additional power to bind a community of believers to each other. The shared relationship to God in worship provides the basis of unity for a shared mission in the world as God's people. The mission of the church has its roots in the worship of God in the church. From the prayers of the congregation come the power and direction for the work of the church in service in the world.

Prayer Makes a Difference to the World

*P*rayer makes a difference beyond the Christian and the church. It makes a difference to the world. The individual Christian in whom the Holy Spirit is at work makes a difference. In the words of Per-Olof Sjogren:

> So it is a good thing that there are people in whose heart Christ dwells. Even one person who has in his heart not a den of thieves but a temple where Christ dwells is an immeasurable blessing for any home, or group, or community. That person carries a lighted candle, the beams of which shine on all whom he meets, on all with whom he has to do. It is not he who shines on the others about him; it is Christ shining in and through him.

Beyond this, the prayer itself affects the world. Our prayers make a positive contribution to reality. There is considerable evidence that in the interconnectedness of all reality, our prayers for others and for the world make a difference to those for whom we pray.

Prayer Makes a Difference to God

*A*nd our prayers make a difference to God. When we pray, we make a way for God's grace to be active in our lives. We provide an opportunity for God's saving, healing, whole-making work in us. As we offer ourselves as God's instruments in the world, God can work not only in us but through us.

Our petitions and intercessions influence God's activity. We do not change God's vision of the ideal possibilities for the creation. But we can affect what God does in a particular concrete situation. God hears all of our prayers and takes them all into account. Our prayers are answered. Many are answered just as we ask them. Others are not. To some of the petitions, the answer may be "No." Other petitions need to be matured and purified in the dialogue of prayer before they can be answered in the context of God's active benevolence toward the whole creation.

How God answers prayer is sometimes beyond our thoughts, and God's ways are not our ways (Isa. 55:8–9). But there is an unending parade of witness to answered prayer. In response to prayer, circumstances change; problems untangle; tensions ease; a clear conviction emerges about an alternative accompanied by the kind of peace and joy that only God can give; a new idea or perspective lights up the mind; fresh courage, calm, comfort, or hope emerges; a nudge to do something is felt; a new desire appears; a temptation diminishes or is conquered; a soul is strengthened; a door opens. God acts in response to what we ask.

And beyond this, some people are so bold as to suggest that God is enriched by our sharing in prayer, that as we express adoration and thanksgiving and share ourselves in confession, petition, intercession, and dedication—as we rest in God's presence in contemplation—we even contribute to God's pleasure! Is it any wonder that Christians have understood prayer to be a part of God's will for our lives?

During the last week of this study, create your own order of prayer. Drawing on your own experience, scripture, and the liturgical resources of the church, create a prayer experience to share with your study group, or to use alone, that makes possible your openness to God and with God.

Perhaps you can begin a long-range program of reading the scripture. Two popular patterns merit your consideration.

1. Follow a daily lectionary. The lectionary suggests three scripture lessons for each day for a year that begins on the first Sunday in Advent. Over the year, major portions of scripture will be covered. The passages will relate to the seasons of the church year—Advent, Christmas, Easter, and Pentecost. Many ministers preach from a lectionary. This might be a way to link your personal devotional reading to the themes highlighted in the corporate worship of your congregation.

2. Choose one or two books from the Bible and read one or two chapters from each during the week. For example, you might begin with the Psalms and the Gospel according to John. Studying the background on these books before beginning to read them devotionally can help you understand the context of what you are reading. A wide variety of Bible study resources can help you know what scholars have learned about the material you are reading. This may stimulate you to hear more than you might otherwise discern in your

reading. Beware, however, of getting sidetracked into doing nothing but objective Bible study. Let the Spirit speak to you through the scriptures as you pray with them.

3. Consider the continuing use of a prayer journal in which you record your prayers. This will help you see how your prayers are growing and appreciate how your prayers are answered.

Bloom, Anthony. *Beginning to Pray.* Mahwah, N.J.: Paulist Press, 1982.

———. *Living Prayer.* Springfield, Ill.: Templegate Publishers, 1975.

Bohler, Carolyn Stahl. *Opening to God.* Nashville, Tenn.: Upper Room Books, 1996.

Dunnam, Maxie. *The Workbook of Living Prayer.* Nashville, Tenn.: Upper Room Books, 1994.

Forsyth, Peter Taylor. *The Soul of Prayer.* Bellingham, Wash.: Regent College, 1993.

Fosdick, Harry Emerson. *The Meaning of Prayer.* Nashville, Tenn.: Abingdon Press, 1987.

Foster, Richard J. *Prayer: Finding the Heart's True Home.* San Francisco: Harper San Francisco, 1992.

Leech, Kenneth. *True Prayer: An Invitation to Christian Spirituality.* San Francisco: Harper San Francisco, 1986

Lewis, C. S. *Letters to Malcolm: Chiefly on Prayer.* Orlando, Fla.: Harcourt Brace, 1973.

Merton, Thomas. *Contemplative Prayer.* New York: Doubleday, 1971.

The Way of a Pilgrim: And a Pilgrim Continues His Way. Translated from the Russian by R. M. French. San Francisco: Harper San Francisco, 1991.

Martha Graybeal Rowlett lives in California and is an ordained clergywoman in The United Methodist Church. Her early professional focus concerned Christian education and leadership development.